Natasha Illum Berg

All Will Be Well

Letters to My Daughter

SAGA Egmont

All Will Be Well: Letters to My Daughter

Original title: *I Merubjergets regnskygge: Breve til min datter*

Original language: Danish
Cover image: Skypaths and Shutterstock
Copyright ©2021, 2023 Natasha Illum Berg and SAGA Egmont

ISBN: 9788727250328

1. POD edition

www.sagaegmont.com
Saga is a subsidiary of Egmont. Egmont is Denmark's largest media company and fully owned by the Egmont Foundation, which donates almost 13,4 million euros annually to children in difficult circumstances.

For Mink.
Loved fiercely and unconditionally.

The eternity of non-existence, as it was before we were born, surely, is no shorter than the one that we encounter again, after death. We fear the non-existence that comes after life, but rarely consider the completely improbable, the quite unbelievable fact, that we somehow managed to take form and step out of nothingness for some time. The life we are given is an exception to the rule.

YEAR ZERO

FEBRUARY

At home. Oldonyo sambu, northern Tanzania.
I have discovered the speck of you, at the line of the slightly
crooked horizon.

APRIL

As for you, I never knew how much I had missed you. Now I
find it hard to wait for your arrival. To see your face, for the
first time.

There are some things I must write now, saying them later,
could become difficult. Also, if I don't say them now, I may
forget, or maybe, when the time would have been just right, I
can't. People die, or worse, they get caught up in things less
important and put them aside indefinitely. I don't think we
should take that risk. It is bad enough that I will not have

time enough here to discuss matters with you, when you have lived to the full.

As I sit here on my isolated hill in northern Tanzania and wonder who you will become, I look out through my tent doors. Our neighbours, who live in a boma on the next hill, a few kilometres away, are from the Waarusha tribe. When the chiefs heard you are on your way, they and some of the warriors slaughtered a goat just outside. We drank some of its still warm blood, to celebrate your coming arrival.

May the generosity, the respect, the life, death and love in this action, give you power through the years that you are about to own on this earth.

Forgive me for my weakness if sometimes, on these pages, I portray myself in a better light than what is palatable. Forgive me again, for my vanity, if I paint a darker picture of myself, than what is true.

Only *Mungu porini*, as the almighty one is called in Swahili, if you believe in the God of the bush, knows how you will feel about me later.

I do know, that I will love you fiercely and show you what I imagine to be true, whilst also squeezing as much life as possible out of my own time-orange here. It seems some people think it's natural that a mother should give up all manners of things vital to her, for the sake of the child. I cannot afford that, and neither can you. No human is strong enough to not resent a little that thing or person whom she thinks put a stop to her. No, I will not offer you such a devastating and false generosity. Instead, I will take your hand and show you where I found the beauty that made me make my choices. Give you keys and seeds and tales from the life I have lived so far, and share with you the plans I have for future adventures.

I will try to ignite your ember with mine.

But I say it, while I can say still it loudly and without feeling shame: I am sorry for what mistakes I did as a mother. Knowing the depth of my intentions now, however, I am sure could not have done better.

APRIL

For almost forty years of my life, you were not. That is a long time of my existence. I will have to be reasonably lucky to call that "half of my life." The doctors tell me that you will arrive in about the same month of the year as what I am in as far as a woman's childbearing age goes: mid-November.

I was born in Northern Europe. To me November was once the month of change, crisp mornings, a few tall hours of light and the odd puffed up bird, who was tough enough, or dumb enough, to have stayed after all the others left. When I was a child, this was the time to pick up the last of the walnuts in their black, rotting wraps, from under soggy leaves. The traversing cold, sideways crabbing, scratching its way through rocks and trunks and stone walls, leaning precariously against windows, nibbling into the edges of the last few leaves still clinging on.

To a child in Tanzania, the Novembers of my childhood, will seem like nonsense. To you November will be the beginning of the sweltering equatorial heat. The short rain's "machine gun popping" on corrugated iron roofs, and the ground coughing up clouds of flying ants, hundreds of wings misting the air. In the month of your birthday, you won't be seeing the winter-sallow, mute Scandinavians, begrudgingly having entered the half-year tunnel of darkness. Instead, it will be perspiring dark faces, filled with either intense relief or worry about the rains. It will be the storms and the hungry field mice shooting past like grey, or striped bullets in our kitchen. The blue sky turning to rolling black and then back to clear blue again, in the course of two hours. Your birthday might very well be the day the rains bring the dust devils down and away for the rest of the year.

Here, November is the month that will either save the maize, or make wilted half-grown plants into cattle fodder. It is a month filled with much emotion, not like so many of the middle months that just slip by.

I will hunt fewer buffalo over the next few years, but still I will hunt them. By mid November, my hunting season will be over. I will be firmly here with you until next season that starts in July. All day writing at my desk.

MAY

Oldonyo sambu, Tanzania, where we live, is dry, like a desert. It is a place of broad yellow dust storms. A month before the rains, the kitchen table will again be covered by fine volcanic dust, just two hours after it has been wiped off.

When I moved to this foothill of Mount Meru, a bit more than a decade ago, I planted our house in this stormy desert. Twice, a storm broke the big glass pane by my bed, that turns towards the mountain. Three times, a part of the roof flew off. A tornado yanked chunks of makuti out of it, twirling them upwards and away, as if we were sitting on an upside down bathtub drain. I planted the trees that have finally grown around our tented home. Every single one of them. Every bush too. It has calmed the dust storms a little. I don't think the glass will break again.

I put out water for the birds. They started coming after a few years. We put out a bit more water each dry season now. The feathered arrivals are growing in numbers and frequency of visits. From high up and fighting the wind, they glide down sideways, aiming for the silver fluid glittering in the vast yellow dryness surrounding us. Crows, white-naped ravens and all manners of smaller birds sail in on the wind and land with a bump, or a whisper. The augur buzzard only sits on the dead tree further away, looking for moles and mice. At night the owl touches down on the makuti roof with a thud, his hooting at the silence only punctured by distant drumming, the blowing of kudu horn. The hyenas call and moan every night as they run past outside. Each time their trotting steps hits the ground hard, their voice distorts a little. I wake up in the night and listen to them. Their voices are all different. I try to figure out how many there are and make up names for them and tell you about them.

My whole life, all seasons have been marked and accepted through the arrival and departure of animal song and animal movement. Especially birds. I would be quite lost if birds were not here to remind me where I am in the world, and in the year. When I was a child and the cranes returned from Africa to us in Sweden, or the Lapwing darted around whining about it all, spring was again trusted by those of us who had heard it. Only by those who had heard it. Your grandfather, *babu* in Swahili, would sit at the end of our long kitchen table and shake his head and click his tongue at the human animal. He would laugh and tell my sister and me that some people didn't notice the sounds that filled the skies and fields and forests around them, or in their gardens. Some of my favourite voices then were red deer, larks, cranes and lapwings. Now hyenas, lions, leopards are familiar chatter I love falling asleep to, like a child falling asleep to the muffled talk of adults in the next room. Hyenas, I am quite sure, will be one of yours. They serenade your beginnings every night up here.

You can never feel lonely again once you stop taking the importance of your own species too seriously. There is not a hope that an oak tree, a fig, or a baobab can not easily lift up from you, once you have told it to the ever gossiping leaves. As for birds, I always found that the ones that migrate don't mind carrying whispers of sadness — to dump them into the nearest ocean for you.

JUNE

There inside my belly you do not have a chance to see your mother. Maybe you will see this something sticking to your bellybutton, and the warm pink walls that surround you. There is also a constant thump, thump in your world. At times it is faster, at times it slows down. A thumping drumroll count-down, bringing you closer to the next stage with each beat.

Later, when looking back at your time in my belly, you cannot make any sense of it, even remember any of it. All that seems so absolutely adamant and fixed one moment is gone and forgotten the next.

From this place, where I am now, again, you will be ignorant to the next stage. This one we call death. Though we talk of death at length out here, and have for thousands of years, we know no more of it than you know now of the shape of your mother's face.

From one belly to the next, none the wiser of where you have been, or where you are going, or where you have arrived to, that is how it goes.

We both hear the muffled sounds from the next place, the muddled clues we catch from the other side of the wall we are pushing our ear up against. The sounds you hear are from a coming life, the sounds I hear are from the coming death. The whole spectacle of a life is a bit like a bullfight. We know the parts: how it starts and how it ends. The question is how well we use the time in the middle. Also, how brave we are at fighting and equally facing it all, when the inevitable comes towards us. Both when we step into life and when we step into death.

So my efforts to describe this life outside my belly to you, are as useless as the dead trying to reach me in life. But I cannot resist the temptation of using a few seconds on describing to you one out of a thousand kaleidoscope angles of reality out here.

Earth is a fairly round rock twisting and turning and flying through an infinitely large space. At its centre is a ball of fire. To you, it will seem like a rather still and cool place. You will not burn your fingers on it when you pick something up that you dropped on the ground. Reaching out your hand will often find cool water, and the ground though it is not so far from the ball of fire at its core, is often so lukewarm or cold that it's easy to forget it's there. It seems, though we know better now, that the sun comes and goes and the moon comes and goes and the stars come and go, and on this we base one of our favourite illusions: time. We had to make these things up: time, and Thursdays and Saturdays, so it didn't just all seem so very mad and confusing on this merry-go-round, that is spinning so fast that we are never sure what or where or who we are. In relation to us, other objects out there, like the moon, are slower and it is us who are spinning deliriously and round, round like a lapdog to the sun. Still, we have told ourselves that we have quite the bigdog importance, anyway. I could talk of all of that with many more words, but it is not so relevant, for this is our home with all of its quirkiness and merry-go-round madness, and we are quite happy to be here. To you it will all seem calmer than what I just described. For, we are so small that almost everything seems big to us. This modestly sized planet we live on appears massive to us. People get lost and die from thirst or hunger, even fear, by just walking in the wrong direction when picking mushrooms in what might really, relatively speaking, be a backyard. There is not much use in thinking about what the really big areas in the universe are, for luckily you are one of us small creatures, and to you this planet will be quite enough to explore for the rest of your life. I would rather explain to you what it has so far been to me, to be one of these creatures here on this spinning rock.

I adore the mind-boggling array of patterns and forms and the different beating hearts. They look so very dissimilar. One has long horns on its head, another has them coming out of its mouth, there is one massive fishlike creature that has a

long horn sticking out from its nose. This last one only lives
in water and would die if you brought it up to the hill, where
we will live. Some have fuzzy hair to their ankles, others don't
even have ankles. Then there is the bizarre notion that we eat
each other. Have you ever heard of such a strange thing?
Some of us cut the skin off and the bones out, and then eat
the other. Others just eat it as it comes naturally. It tastes fine
too, if you ask me.

One of my favourite things in the world is the creatures
who floats in the air above us. It's the birds again. You have to
admit it. It is spectacular what they can do. However much
you and I would try, we could not fly, as it is called. We have
invented machines we can sit inside to try to be like them, but
it is not the same. We stick to the ground with our two feet
and think of being up in the air like all of those creatures up
there. It seems freer somehow. Instead, we stand like Maasai
spears from the ground, stick out in all directions, all the way
around the globe. From afar, now that there are so many of
us, the planet must look like a sleeping hedgehog. Still, we
dream of being like them - the birds - so much that some of
us say that the best of us get wings as the ultimate present,
after death. That is how much we would like to be like them.
Imagining that we might get wings after this life, even makes
it easier for some people to keep walking.

Not a single one of us - not anyone I have heard of at least
- would deny that all that grows here and all the different
shapes of landscapes and the way the sun looks down upon
us with its clear burning eye in the day, or the way the moon
casts its ever-changing face at us, is the most spectacular we
can imagine.

Some of the most learned people have, since as far back as
we know, tried to write its beauty, or paint its colours, or
make its music. We buy many things here, but there are few
things we will pay a higher price for than when a painter has
caught the essence of nature on a canvas, be that of the
human nature, or that of a landscape. There are few things we
remember for longer than a writer who managed to capture
with a few words the very same thing. And the composer,
who gets even halfway to bringing the emotion a nightingale
can produce, will awaken the highest admiration one man
can feel for another. Do you see how hopeful that is? That we
can love our home, our earth, to such a degree that nothing
brings greater joy than successful attempts at imitating
fragments of it and putting it down on paper or canvas. So
much do we love nature that we want to keep looking at
horses running through the morning mist, albeit inside a
gilded frame, while we are having our breakfast. So much do
we long for the emotion the lark evoked in our childhood
summers, that we have music fill our winter dark rooms to
produce faintly the same feeling. Words can make prison
walls crumble for a few moments if they capture the emotion
of ocean waves hitting a boat.

The first things we read to children, the stories I too will
tell you when you arrive, will mostly be about animals and
seas and forests. Like other children here, not long after you
can say *mama* and *baba*, you will imitate the sound of cows
and chickens and lions. Only later will you speak human
sentences.

Mysteriously, however, it seems we only truly adhere,
admit, succumb, to this world's beauty when we are close to

either side of eternity. We only seem acutely aware of nature's superior importance to us, having just stepped out of it, or on our way re-entering it.

I cannot explain to you what happens to man's sense of relativity between that which matters versus that which does not, during that long middle bit of a lifetime. It seems there are many years where most of it is quite forgotten.

JUNE

There are things to love in big cities too. Culture, for instance. Culture is spectacular and we must have it injected if we want to learn how to question and expand.But this is not where you will be brought up.

In cities we will find the theatre, the literature, the museums, the exhibitions, the meeting of cultures, science, protest and architecture, but they are also, in some ways, dulling, frightening places.

Away from nature and surrounded by concrete, we squander our tools – mediocre, primitive tools they are maybe – but never the less the only ones we truly mastered.

From here we throw rocks at our own reflection in a lake, when no other true mirrors exist.

Walls outside walls, outside walls, with urbanised man shrinking and rattling in the centre, like a winter walnut.

Roots cannot, cannot, find place from here.

I have just heard that half of the world's population live in cities. Imagining that you are about my age when you read this, the city dweller must be the most common human by now.

At a first glance, it could seem like a good thing only, that people congregate and leave nature to doing what nature does best on its own, but at least in some ways it is quite the opposite. The fully urbanised man is a creature who had lost touch with nature. Losing touch means losing reality. Already now the amount of people I meet, who do not seem at home in nature, is staggering. People who fear harmless, peaceful beetles going about their business and who could never conceive of eating a berry from a bush before having washed it first. People who have lost the understanding of the core of their own existence, who regard and poke at nature without it ever dawning on them that they are looking at their own intestines. All this distancing from nature is a bit like turning the volume between brain and spinal cord way down, and then to watch our arms and legs move, without understanding how or why.

JUNE

Today, your father and I found out that you will be a girl.

What a perfectly wonderful thing that is.

I have always been utmost content to be one, so I am very pleased for you.

I do not have too many ideas attached to how a girl should live, as opposed to a boy. In my family, for as many generations as I care to know about, women always choose the roads of their desires. They lived how they pleased to and professionally did what they wanted, simply because they saw it as their natural right.

On my side of the family, anybody who might oppose to a woman's choice of profession or lifestyle, or try to dirty it for looking as free as that of a man's, will simply be regarded as curiosity, a comical and uncivilised hindrance that must be moved out of the way, with calm and swift insistence.

There is no need to demand your right to follow your chosen road. Just take it. It is no one's place to give permission. Demanding leads to the belief that something is not already yours. We just go in any direction we like, with respect and conviction insistently chipping away at any obstacles with hard work and steady flying. Equality between the sexes, of course, does not mean being the same, it merely means having the same possibilities, freedom and the same say. We don't confuse courtship with demeaning behaviour. You wouldn't kill a butterfly for landing in your jam, now would you?

I will tell you this, however, and I am sorry to do so; that albeit the common everyday professional male chauvinism is lessening, the core chauvinism of the patriarchy we live in remains untouched. I am talking of the core male vision glasses that are stitched firmly onto our faces. Yours too.

Anything — from what is a good wine, to a fine painting, to a good style of writing literature — was defined by men so long ago that we are now totally and utterly immersed in these standards, all of us. Men and women alike.

This subtle, yet all-encompassing, "core chauvinism" creates little, if any, discomfort and is invisible and wholly enveloping and natural, like the air we breathe. It simply looks like truth.

Humanity is far from having found a way to break this bond. For our collective idea of good and bad, whether in morals or in tastes, have already been completely and firmly established through thousands of years of a cultural patriarchate. We are pickled in a set of rules now so deeply embedded in all our collective take on reality that neither sex understands how to see it from another angle. We are jellied stiff in the juice of our history, absolutely and completely beyond critical opinion by any of us.

When you realise that the world still ticks to the clock of the historical power of one sex, it is a complete misunderstanding to be angry with men about it. It is no more the fault of the men than the women who live today that we are here now. Men or women are only a product of generations upon generations of how the men and women who brought them up allowed them, or told them, to be. It is as much the fault of those who took the power as it is to those who did not rise up against in or support those who did.

Men did not raise men, more than they raised women, and women did not raise women, more than they raised men. If anything, women did most of the raising. We are here because these premises were accepted by our entire society for a very long time.

Promise me to not become one of those women who does not support other women in their fight to open doors for themselves. This strange jealousy is schoolgirl behaviour and equal-opportunity suicide.

There is only one thing worse than a male chauvinist and that is a female male chauvinist. It is very much because women stop women, that all doors are not ajar for us yet. Women are good at keeping women back.

Far too many of our sex will still throw their loyal friends of twenty years overboard for a man who has just walked into their lives (at least until they are single again). Men rarely do that. This is not because the man loves less or is colder, but because he understands he can have both deep passion and love for a woman and remain true to his individual person.

Compromise is a word used a lot by women, who give up their jobs and friends and dreams to be with their partner. To me, that does not sound like compromise. To me, it is not a testament to do with the level of passion and love she might feel for him, but how little ambition she has.

I adore, admire and love many men as lovers, friends, brothers and fathers in all ways, but equality between the sexes is a complicated thing.

In any kind of equality of the sexes, whether the simpler or core kind, there is nothing innocent about trying to break any of the granite hard laws we collectively put upon ourselves. It is an act of violence. A trespassing into the calm of repetition and order of both men and women.

When you try, there is a lot of fear and aggression from both sexes. Breaking old ways makes some things disappear forever. Some people's entire role in society seems threatened and at risk of passing away into obscurity, or appears less admirable. To some people, when they meet a woman carrying this new sort of defiant freedom, it gives them the frightening and infuriating sense that they themselves will now never again be taken so seriously in society. This new insolent and noisy person smears egg all over their place in history. They fear they will not quite be understood in the same way, in this new light. And they are right, they will not.

To plant something, to uproot something else, always leads to getting dirt under your nails.

Strong, very independent girls with opinions were never entirely forgiven during my life so far. Neither by women, nor by men.

The clean, silent, shallow breathing people who sit still in the boat will always have the steadiest, most harmonious lives. Less fucked up chaos. They have one conviction and they are all perfectly united in its mode of operandi—to do nothing about anything. They will always have more energy left over than you when the sun sets and don't have blood gushing from their broken noses.

Being involved, breaking ground, taking affair, speaking up, is asking for a continued stream of slaps. Passivity, on the other hand, is the premeditated, lazy scalpel-cut, taken to the throat of fairness, happiness and self-worth and makes you lousy company to yourself.

Whether you choose passivity or uproar, there will be damage. You only get to choose which kind.

Of course, nothing is to say things would have been hugely different, or better, if women had had the upper hand from the beginning of time. All races, and sexes, of all animals, get rather silly when given too much power.

Best would be if men and women understood sticking together, so we can start discussing our future as a species here instead. Soon it might become painfully apparent to everyone, through mass disease, or nature disasters, that we are an unimportant animal to earth, in fact one that is more than dispensable. That will be a bit of a kick in the teeth. One we need to handle together. Educating women and giving them the right to their own bodies might be our saviour, for the survival of the human species. Educate women and watch us control our own population before disease and weather does it for us, in a much more unpleasant way.

I will explain to you in time what education and the right over your own body means to you. The key to our future here is in your hands too, my girl.

JULY

I have no soil to give you. "Clump clay on your boots heaviness" is the most soothing painkiller for not having wings.

A part of you, be it small or big, must be feet planted in the ground, dirt between your toes and fingers, leaves in your hair, when you are a child of mine.

You have been with me in the bush before, when you were more biology than specifically a human. Whilst you were still a secret. You will not know, for you were not much more than a tadpole then.

From in there you have already experienced waking up at about 04.30 every morning. Maybe you have heard it when one of the camp staff comes to my tent with tea and calls my name and pours hot water into the basin outside for me to wash my face. I mumble something in return, a "thank you" or a sound, to make him understand I am awake now. Always awake before the day, when we are in the bush. A few minutes later, I get up and sometimes just step into the same clothes that I left on the floor next to the camp-bed the previous evening. I first reach for my leather belt with my ammunition holder in the light of the kerosene lamp, which is the only light I prefer early in the morning. The pocket watch with a compass that my mother gave me years ago is always on me. I prefer long trousers and long-sleeved shirts, for I know I will crawl on the ground at some stage during the day, or pull myself forward on my stomach. I always want to be close, so I'm crawling, sliding forward or backward, getting up a tree, or crouching down through thorn-bushes.

I open my small leather ammunition box that my grandfather carried with him on his expeditions at the beginning of the nineteen hundreds. Inside the lid is a note from my mother, your grandmother, that I read in the dim light before I go out into the world, every morning. It says to remember that she loves me and that I am strong. I take out what I need and close it again. Reach for my only gun, Ishmael, and my old worn binoculars and my ridiculously torn hat, and go to the mess for breakfast. I like those things that have been with me for so many years. It seems to me they stood the test of time and that convinces me I did too. They were always watching, steadily growing older, following my journey with tangible patience and support, until I too showed signs of having travelled far.

I miss you so much, and I miss being in the bush a little too. Seems I'm swelling more and more every day with "waitingness."

JULY

You are about to arrive in this world that I have been acquainted with for forty years.

Fate would have it you are born a child, meaning the offspring of a human being. You are one of the nearer 9,000,000 species on this planet. Though you don't genetically differ from most of them all that much, and are closely related to most of them, your experiences here will be quite unusual. I don't know what it feels like to be a bee, or a baobab tree, or a blade of grass, but you are born into a tribe that displays, in numerous ways, though they may say something different, that they think we are the king species on this planet.

How could we think differently?

We have the power to end almost any other species we like, and have done so frequently. No animal has, of yet, shown any ability to understand what we have done to them, let alone revenge themselves. Mankind has also accomplished things we cannot but regard as miraculous. We have created, with our own minds and hands, things that occasionally change some of nature's courses. Temporarily, at least. This has made us measure ourselves against nature itself, even more than against the other species. In fact, we blindly don't even see the other species as competition any more. How can we do anything but admire ourselves more than the rest of the animals? We are the only creature here who can challenge nature enough to make a dying child, or indeed a dying animal, live despite nature's judgement, using medicines we invented. I, for one marvel at the thought of a journey that started when man picked up the first tool, has led us to being able to walk on the moon. Or that we can perform open heart surgery, where we literally pause a person, while we work on repairing the very ember that keeps him in the realm of the living.

Each time we conquer a disease, or keep other threatening natural factors at bay, and make our lives longer, we feel larger, slightly less intimidated by the merciless course of nature. Each time we invent machines that can send us to unknown planets in an endless universe, or others that can look into a world infinitely smaller than what can be seen with the naked eye, we feel more in control. Knowledge makes us feel sturdier. That is, in the places where we don't just ignore the knowledge we find (we know about and are successful at preventing disease, but we also know about and still propel ourselves closer to the 6th mass extinction.) The prevention of yet a disease gives us hope of immortality. By pushing back death, a sense of divinity flutters by and lands in our midst, as a sign that even meaninglessness can be conquered by man soon. For many are convinced that immortality is the opposite of meaninglessness.

So, congratulations, you will be born a future queen, just by being the child of a human, but I am sorry, you are still just a top-notch monkey.

It would be madness to not pursue where your mind's curiosity and hunger takes you, and may that desire take you to pinnacles hereto unseen.

You see, nature, entirely oblivious to the human scruples, will happily let you carve out any heightened place for yourself above the other creatures, if so you please. Nature is quite deaf and mute and will do nothing to discourage you when we climb that rickety pedestal high in the sky, from where we shout out your superiority. Nature will only push you down once you have properly compromised its balance. Have no doubt that it then will.

AUGUST

When I listen to people speak of nature, I rarely recognise it to be the same as the one that I have lived with and known so well, my entire life.

We should not eat flesh, death is like a mistake, and God think like humans, they imply.

And I think: up there above the canopy high and mighty man sees only thin air. Down by the root of the trees, things are different.

The only God I know is nature. It slips back and forth between the tree trunks, cutting throats with quick precision one moment, bringing slow moss to grow itself thick with unending patience the next. All done with the same unsentimental perfection.

AUGUST

It is damned hot here. I am sitting in a two metre in radius, bell shaped, canvas tent, just twenty-five metres away from our little home in Oldonyo sambu. I am trying to write. My ankles are swollen. We don't fit behind the table anymore.

I am also trying not to think about why I cannot reach across the short space of air between your father and I. I am numbed by the sadness I just felt from holding him in an embrace a moment ago. It was like holding a struggling creature, a beautiful, angry creature, who constantly tries to change shape and colour, as if he cannot decide if he wants to stand out clearly, or camouflage completely. He can bite hard too.

A tingling and choking sensation at once creeps up across my chest and lodges at the suprasternal notch. It is the embodiment of something dying. I try to lift my head a little and straighten my back. I try to become angry. None of it works. There is no anger. "Piss off then," I say out loud to the tears, "so go!".

SEPTEMBER

Not wanting you to feel the sadness that is surging through my body and into you, I try to think about something else. I have written a song for you today, and I sing it to you. I try to fill my mind with our first big adventure together. A few weeks ago, we came back from our first long safari together. You and I walked across a small stretch of Zambia and a big stretch of Namibia. You were four to five months before ETA. We guided ten physically challenged men and women on a long walk most able people could never do. My mission was to get us safely past animals and through the landscape. Theirs was to support each other mentally and physically through the hours of the day and night. I accepted the job as "expedition leader" because for the last 25 years I had listened so many times to perfectly fit people complaining that they were unable to follow their dreams, with only pathetic excuses in their way. Here was a group of people who had the best excuses in the world, but refused to listen to them. Their passion was stronger than their bodies. The price of our

adventure was that it had to be filmed for television, but we
didn't mind that too much.

Metal arms and legs, weak eyes and wheelchairs on balloon
tyres we set out to cross swamps, savanna and the desert.
There was the gentle heart of a boy with cerebral palsy and
limbs that had to be mentally commanded into action by
each step, tears sometimes running down his cheeks. One
man's feet were where shins should have been and the
long-legged shadows of his childhood fears and despairs
stuck to his heels in the morning sun. There were shoulders
with no arms. Feet holding a fork gentler than most hands. A
man whose burning heart outshone any flame that had ever
devoured his skin and limbs. Ten powerful minds challenging
ten compromised bodies. We walked every day, the whole
day, for a month. We started gently at the Caprivi strip and
headed for the skeleton coast.
    Already, you have felt the slow movement of travelling far
on foot across Africa.
    You made your presence known, though you were not
much bigger than a pear. Every morning, like the rest, I
packed up my bedding and took down my tent before
breakfast. You secured extra room for you in my belly, by
jealously making me throw anything not-you from my gut
and into a bush before dawn. It was a routine we had, starting
at 05.30. - Get up, throw up, pack up. No one, but the doctor
who was there to support the ten travellers, knew you were
there, until the last days. It was our delicious secret. We found
places to talk in the afternoon, in the shade of an acacia tree,
or on the other side of a dune. When we walked through

Etosha national park, I whispered to you where we were and what we were looking at and what I saw. You were the only person who ever truly understood that it wasn't the lion spoor that posed an indirect threat. It was all the sign of rhinos. I was upset that I didn't have Ishmael, my gun, but one that I had borrowed.

For a few weeks we had a privacy that we could not hold on to much longer, buttons beginning to revolt against secrecy. The Swedish doctor panicked when I told him we had a half-baked passenger with us. I made sure I only told him, once we had left our starting point at Victoria falls, because people strange to Africa always worry so unreasonably much. After I had told him, he immediately made several satellite telephone calls and I could hear him fretting about diseases that could happen to us. We laughed. You are not exactly the first child to be baked in Africa.

It was graceful to see people do so much that others had told them they could not. We walked for eight hours a day, literally pushing and pulling kilometre after kilometre forward, through sand and mud. You and I carried one of the bravest men I have ever met on our backs up a dune, as his legs could not bend. We waded through rivers, laughed and mercilessly pushed everyone forward strictly, while secretly admiring all the people on the trip.

At nightfall, you and I walked a distance away from all the others to breathe in peace and put our tent up. Far enough that you too could hear the muffled roar of lions and buffalo grazing. Also, so that I could have a bucket wash and put on my kanzu in peace while standing in the open, which is the best way to wash. We were wearing my blue flowing kanzu

when I had to run out and scare naughty elephants away
from camp in the middle of the night.

After a month, and only two of the participants having
given up after a very brave and hard fight, we ended up at the
Skeleton Coast.

Now the two of us are back home in Tanzania. Buttons
and zips have quite left us behind and we seem to both be
outgrowing ourselves a bit more every day.

SEPTEMBER

I am here in my writing tent on the hill. This is my office now.
My large desk, that to others might look more like a big
kitchen table, has been prepared to become your changing
table. I got it ready today while your father was in town.
Stacks of clothes and nappies and towels now lay where I
used to have my dictionaries, my mountains of papers, my
gun cleaning kit and my eleven notebooks. I have written
four books at that desk. Maybe I will write more at it again,
when you are older. A local carpenter made it about thirteen
years ago from a broken bit of mninga timber we confiscated
from poachers.

I was down south from here then, living in a small tent by
the Wami River for a few months, doing a game count in an
area considered for tourism. At night, the elephants would
come down and eat the sweet fruits that fell from the palm
trees, and drink from the river. Their trunks or feet would
touch the guide-ropes, and now and again one side of the tent
would collapse. I would lie inside and hope the elephants
would leave or at least move a little further away, before the
collapse of the other side of the tent would pancake me.

In the evenings when I came back from the bush and in the mornings before I went out, I would sit at that table. It already served as a desk then, and a dinner table, being the only table around in kilometres. In the beginning, I had some guinea-fowl that I had bought in the nearest village, keeping me company. They ran back and forth in front of where I was sitting, but one night they flapped away from their branch, scared off by a honey badger, maybe. They must have landed in the river. I never saw them again. There were no more guineafowl-egg omelettes for a long while after that.

A wild-eyed, mad haired fisherman, who smoked copious amounts of weed and swore that no crocodile could ever touch his flesh, arrived one day at my spot on the river bank. He tied his canoe just there in front of where I was sitting drinking my tea and came up to that very table. I asked him from which village he had come. He answered me he preferred to live on his own. He only went to villages now and again to swap fish for tomatoes and onions.

After a certain amount of conversation, we agreed he would come to my little camp when he had caught enough fish to sell. At first he came once a week, then twice. Eventually, he slept under a nearby little tree of his choice, on a more permanent basis.

He took it upon himself to bring me tea in the afternoon. He would, he said, play his marimba softly in my camp very often, if I promised to do something about his gonorrhoea. I agreed.

Every afternoon after that, he first brought me half of the catch of the day, if there was any, then tea. A moment after I had paid for the fish - exactly long enough that my tea had cooled sufficiently for me to drink it - he came back, turned around and pulled his shorts down. I stuck the thick needle, that looked more like it had been made for a horse, into his buttock, and injected a medicine he had brought. It continued like this for a few weeks.

Then it continued like this for a few more months still, only now without the injection, and I could drink my tea while it was still warm. We talked little, but just accepted each other's nearness, like two plants randomly growing side by side on the same riverbank.

The whole day he was out fishing, while I was out in the bush doing my game count, or sitting at my table writing, or laying in my tent reading. When he put up his nets near my camp, I would see him in the middle of the river, diving deeply to untangle his net. He perfectly trusted what the local witch doctor had once told him - namely, that none of the many crocodiles in the river would ever touch his flesh. Starting late afternoon, in what I imagine was a state of half sleep marijuana high, he would play his marimba throughout the rest of the day and most of the night. Like he had promised. It was a very pleasant sound, and he was far away enough that it did not disturb my sleep. To me, it was the sound of perfectly contented solitude in company. The times I woke up in the middle of the night in my little camp, that unbroken stream of music was present. I drifted in and out of it with the ebb and flow of sleep. Sometimes I wondered if he, or indeed the instrument itself, kept playing when he was asleep, too. I never asked him how he could play for so many hours every night, neither did I ever go over in the night to have a look. I did not want to scare him away. I did not want to look too candidly at someone who preferred living amongst life forms that neither spoke nor disturbed him.

This little office tent of mine next to our bigger living tent could not contain that big table, anyway. This tent is just big enough that it fits a small travel desk, a travel trunk, some kind of chaise longue, a mayhem of open books, diaries, photographs, two days' worth of tea and coffee cups and the two trays that Laito brought them on.

The flies gather inside any closed-off space this time of year. In my office too, the flies bottle. The rains are coming anytime now. We are all waiting.

My belly is big. It sits on my body. Round, like a planet. It feels hot and heavy, and the welcome committee here is getting impatient. Seems you are trying to kick your way out of your confinement. I gather you have had enough, too.

I unzip the bottommost part of the tent and roll it up. A tiny breeze slides by my swollen feet. You stop kicking so frantically and stretch, changing the shape of my round stomach into what looks like a giant pawpaw hanging from its stalk of a tree.

SEPTEMBER

Before I became pregnant, I imagined you growing inside me would just feel like a part of my own weave expanding, coming to life. A bit of my pattern, hidden until now, pulled out from an obscure part of me and miraculously, but simply, put in to motion.

But it does not feel like this. You are not a part of my pattern. I know that so clearly now.

I will love you fiercely, but you are not mine. Your life, inside my womb, is not fully developed, yet I can already hear that it has wound up and started its own clock. It ticks separately from mine, at a different pace to mine. And your hands, that swipes across my full moon belly from the inside, are so clearly defined. Your knuckles, sometimes the heel of your foot, stick out, as to try to push through me. Already you have your very own lines defying mine.

I will have to get to know you when you arrive — a new lodger who has already smacked enough rent down onto the table to pay for a slot of history that stretches beyond mine. When you look around with your milky bleary eyes, confused from the daylight, for the first time, I will have to ask you: "Who are you, my love?" And I will have to teach you how to speak, so you can answer. I will have to show you how to tell the difference between wind, darkness and moonlight too, just so that you can do with it all what you want.

It was a surprise to me, that you took root inside me with such matter of course. That you appeared with such absolute certainty. You being inside me does not make me anything like a giver of life, like I thought it would have done. You brought it all with you. Your complete own set of it. What I merely have to do is to deliver you when you are ready.

SEPTEMBER

Your first home is a tiny, hut-like building made of wood and canvas that sits isolated on the top of an arid hill, in the Northern part of Tanzania. Behind it, just a few hundred metres away, is the border of the Mount Meru forest reserve. Below is the Rift Valley. It towers over us, Mount Meru. We are in the rain shadow, on the one crop a year side of the mountain. Most people live on the two crops a year side. You and I and your father live here now. By the time the two of you arrived on this hill, I had already been here for many years.

Your father and I got to know each other, when I was in Europe over a summer. One day, he met me in a café in Copenhagen and told me he was in love. His hands were trembling when he did, and his eyes were deep brown, like that of an elephant. So I made my home his and now we are three in this little place.

Before I moved here to Oldonyo Sambu, I had already lived in East Africa for over ten years. The first five were in Tanzania and the next in Kenya, albeit I always spent the hunting season in Tanzania. When one of the people I have loved most in my life was murdered outside my house in Nairobi, it was time to move away from a place with many people and back to Tanzania completely. With an approximate radius of 45 minutes from Arusha, the safari hub town of Tanzania, I made a circle on a map and drove all the way around that circle, looking for my view. This was where I found it.

When I arrived here, there was nobody else living on this side of the thousand acre farm. There was a farmhouse, down the hill, hidden behind the tall non-indigenous eucalyptus and jacaranda trees, but it was empty, except for a couple of days a month, when the owner came and drank his tea there and then left a few hours later. Down there, erosion, of ground unrooted, unheld, unlived on, had set in already a long time before I arrived. It showed in the grass-free indentations, where pieces of old German machinery had lain idle for years. One by one, they had been carried away in the dark of night, to the jingling sound of Waarusha or Maasai jewellery. Inside the house, erosion showed in the missing tables, the uneven numbered chairs. Machinery and furniture that had been carefully crated and shipped by boat from Europe, in the beginning of the last century, still eroding out through unlocked windows and broken doors.

The farmland itself was uprooting, where the Masai and the Waarusha had let their cattle, sheep and goats graze until nothing but dust was left. The farmhouse was peeled, the land was skinless, and underneath fragile things lifted and blew away for ever, disappeared or evaporated with indifferent ease.

This, I was told, had once been a tightly run dairy farm. All the cows had died years ago and the owner, who had inherited it from his hardworking German mother, had moved closer to the bars of Arusha, only carrying with him one suitcase packed with his own personal erosion.

When I had found my spot, high on the farm, out of sight of anything but mountains, the Rift Valley, and the sky, I drove back to Arusha and searched all the bars in town. Tipped off by one of his acquaintances, I finally found the farm owner in a dark restaurant off the main street, by the clock tower. When I asked him if I could build a canvassed home on his farm, he first answered "yes," then "definitely no, no," to be followed by "why not"? Then, with slight disdain, as if I was about to take something from him he really should have been guarding, but, bitterly, did not have the tenacity to do, he said; "Maybe, let's see,". Then, having reasoned much in the same haphazard, mysterious manner I would come to see he always had, he indicated that our conversation was over.

I couldn't tell if his changing answers were from my lack of understanding, or if it was the blurry answers of alcohol and bangi (marijuana).

One day, he called me and gave his final "yes". When we met me again a few weeks later, he explained with a big, boyish smile that he wasn't a "country bumpkin" and would rather stay in A-town, Arusha. He even produced a contract for leasing four acres on top of one of the hills on the farm.

Then I built a home. Not with my own hands, but with the help of a couple of carpenters and many metres of canvas brought down from Kenya. I made a drawing on the back of an envelope and the very short, curly haired strawberry blonde, local American, and his enormous Mozambican foreman said they could do it.

I wasn't there when the gum-tree poles were brought to the hill, which was as pale and arid as a bald white man's head. I had to be in Europe for a few months. When I came back, I again drove the 50 minutes journey in a constant slow rise from Arusha to the top of my hill, to see what was waiting for me there. My steady old dark green land-cruiser pickup from the seventies, bounced up the hill slowly. There was no house yet, that much was clear, but a big heap of gum tree poles lay stacked one upon the other, maybe still drying.

I saw from a distance a man was sitting on top of them, hatless in the midday sun. I discovered it to be a short man of a very slight frame, with a mild face. He was wearing no adornments and didn't carry a spear, so he was obviously not a Mwaarusha or Maasai. He held out a small hand and introduced himself as Laito. Then he told me that a carpenter had given him a few thousand shillings to guard the wood. For the first time I witnessed him speak and move in that characteristic slow, patient manner, as if he never in his life was in a rush to be anywhere else than exactly where he was. When I asked him for how long he had been there, he told me he had been paid to wait by the wood for five days, but that he had already sat on the pile for three weeks.

From that first day until now, he has been coming and going in our little house here on the hill every day, bar Sundays and holidays, cleaning, washing, feeding the dogs and making tea. In his quiet and gentle way. Every morning he walks up from the nearest village, in his gumboots. When he arrives, he takes them off and walks around for the rest of the day barefoot, doing things in his own slow, meticulous speed and I rarely interfere. He came with the house; he came with my life on the hill, and to me it seemed I could do nothing but accept.

I can hear him now as I write this to you. I think he is downstairs taking the dog baskets outside. He was from the first day the guardian of my solitude and for that, I am immensely grateful. He is not so very good at cleaning and his habits are quite unbreakable, but never have I met a human being who merely by quietly walking in and out of my house, or passing behind my chair when I am working at my desk, can give me the feeling that things are calm and good.

I know now that Laito is from the Sandawe tribe. On the BBC I heard, the other day, that the Wasandawe are part of the oldest human lineage in the world. I told him that and he smiled all the way back to the beginning of mankind, but did not comment.

I know he is looking forward to meeting you, too. I am glad, for he has a kind and gentle soul.

OCTOBER

When I arrived on this hill, I planted some trees and bushes and watched them try to stand up against the wind and drought. The first few years I lived up here, the daylight hours were silent, except for the sound of the strong wind, and the occasional clap and rumble of a thunderstorm.

The morning I lay in bed and heard the first weaver bird land and speak outside, not just pass over like they had always done, I knew all beginnings were possible, for I had made a small, small forest out of a desert.

Some people say; "you should move to a place that already has mature trees there. It takes years before they get big." But I like being the one who plants. I love that feeling of covering the roots with black volcanic soil and stamping the earth down hard to get the air out of there. I enjoy looking at trees growing in fits and bursts after the rains. It makes me feel rich. We all started in a new place together the trees and us, gave ourselves a big chance here, and we are all doing well. It is an everyday testament to time that these trees might keep standing with you once I am in the ground. That is all good and how it should be.

Or maybe I take that for granted because your babu always told me that; "people who have not understood that we plant trees for our children, have not understood a goddamn thing!"

The beauty of nature is the most generous thing there is. It gives itself completely, down to the smallest detail and without a hint of reserve, to anybody who has understood merely to look properly. It is a grain, smaller than what is visible to the naked eye, capable of inflating itself to the size of the infinite, merely at someone's attention. For those who will not see or sense it, it simply stops existing, folds itself away into a great big nothingness.

That invisible grain—is from where you sprang too. Right there in my gut.

OCTOBER

For ten years, it used to be only the hyenas, Laito and I up here on a normal day — and Amadi, my night watchman, snoozing next to his spear behind a bush. Friends would fight their way through the dust storms and come for a visit. Sometimes a leopard got tempted to venture down from the forest on Mount Meru by the alluring smell of my two ridgebacks and an owl landed heavily on my makuti roof. occasionally, groups of morani, men in their warrior-hood, would pass near our tent shouting, singing, drumming and blowing a kudu-horn and wake me up in the middle of the night.

Now that you are in my belly, Amadi frantically throws stones at the owl every evening, the only bird that lands on our roof. He never used to care so much about the owl, but now that you are coming, he will not tolerate it anymore. To the Waarusha, as to most other African tribes, an owl landing on a roof means that someone inside that house will die. I keep telling him not to. He assures me he has stopped, but he is just throwing smaller stones when he thinks I am asleep. I hear the pebbles land on the makuti roof and heavy wings flap off. I have told him that the owl means wisdom to me. He stands there looking very confused every time I tell him to stop throwing stones at them, as if I am trying to tell him that wisdom comes to people only after death. Begrudgingly, he even lets the chameleons live these days, albeit he really thinks I am an idiot for protecting them. At least some he let get away. I don't know how many he kills behind my back. He is only trying to save you from evil.

I lay awake, looking into the cool, clear night. Sometimes with your father's breathing next to me, sometimes not, while you are doing endless somersaults in my belly.

OCTOBER

The only activity on the farm where we are, besides our own, is the morning arrival of local cattle, and the women who go up Mount Meru to collect firewood. The little herdsmen, who some of them are only four years old, arrive first in the mornings. Then the Waarusha women walk past my house in long lines, like colourful soldier ants, pangas on their heads on the way up, bundles of wood on their heads, on the way down.

There are nights, when the particularly warrior-some Mezeeza stays behind with his cattle, after all others have gone home. It is a midnight sport for him to see how many of my newly planted trees his cattle can eat, before he can bring me out from my tent like a hornet, to confront him wielding my torch.

My first three years here, I bought milk from him every day, thinking that it would temper his want for war, but it did not. When for the fourth time he herded his cattle to my house, for no other desperation than to end a warriors peacetime lethargy, Amadi and I took as ransom four of his cows and two of his goats. By this time I knew the rules of the Waarusha and I shouted the going fine for both cows, sheep and goats brought inside someone else's boma, while shining my torch in his sly, uncharacteristically hook-nosed face. He did a few mock charges; pulled his spear out of the ground with a sudden jerk and lifted his panga high before resting it on his shoulder. I was not holding his cattle back from water in times of drought. I had no waterholes that I was stopping his animals from going to. Neither did my grass or the shoots from my trees offer a diet significantly more wholesome than what he could find a few hundred metres away. So that he should kill me seemed reasonably unlikely.

He arrived back the next day and paid up with no more ado with a look of glee in his beady eyes before he took his livestock back. I wondered what I had missed, since he clearly walked off as if he was the victor of the battle. He was not the only perpetrator, but he was by far the most incomprehensibly insistent one.

Even though this is a private farm in a sea of free land, I did many negotiations with the Waarusha since the beginning of being up here. With the chief present and hinting at the powers I had over snakes, my liking for owls and chameleons, expensive fines were paid for trespassing cattle on numerous occasions. Hinting at my witch powers was the only method that seemed to work. After that, most of the Waarusha did not come all the way up to the canvas, but kept their cattle at a respectful distance.

Once a year, I invited the chiefs to come and slaughter and eat a goat with me, and they came with great ceremonial seriousness. Eventually, we started greeting each other in a more friendly manner every time we passed each other on the road.

Now, on my way up and down from our hill, I often fill the car with schoolchildren (who steal sweet things I hide in the backdoor pockets). Patients who need to go to the local hospital get in to my car as well. My favourites are the tiny herds boys who get in with ear-deafening screeches of delight, just to try sitting in a car, and even when it is heading in the opposite direction of where they should be going.

Only Mezeeza has persisted, and I am glad you and I are not the owners of this farm. Every year, a new case opens in the name of Mezeeza. I have opened a few. The owners of the farm have opened a few and I can see four mud-huts from here owned by people who have all opened cases against him.

He is proud to have so many cases against him, and still never goes to court or prison by paying his way out. The intoxicating feelings of power that he gets from being above the law, with the help of corruption, must make him feel like a real man. Every time he got arrested, he comes back one cow less.

Once, I woke up in the middle of the night by the sounds of him and Amadi having a loud fight. I ran out wearing a white kanzu and rubber boots, a torch shining at my face while shouting and screaming like a madwoman. He left his cows behind and ran. Amadi was bleeding from the face, but he proudly assured me that Mezeeza was bleeding too. We pushed his cows down the hill and when we walked up again Amadi was laughing so hard at the whole thing, while talking, that I did not understand what he was trying to explain to me.

As the cows dwindled over time and the court cases against him grew, he still did not look any less pleased with himself. One day, before he took over his brother's cows, his last cow was gone, and he didn't have any means to bribe anyone. All the court cases came rattling down from the shelves at the local judge's office and he was put away for a few months.

I heard that he is out of prison again. I only know from the trick he has done to the owner of the farm this time. I cannot help but admire his sly plans a little. This time, he pushed his cattle all the way into the greenhouses of the farm owners. The farm owner took all the cattle to the police and left it there, telling him he could have it back once he had paid the traditional ransom. Meanwhile, Mezeeza secretly went to the police and paid them off to release the cattle back to him. He then obediently paid the farm owner the ransom and demanded to get the cattle back. When the farm owner went down with him to the police station, of course, the cattle were not there. Having been bribed by Mezeeza first, the police looked the farm owner straight in the eyes and said: "Cattle? What cattle? You brought no cattle to us!!" He then contacted the police in Dar es Salaam and told them he, Mzeeza, a poor Mwaarusha from the slopes of Mount Meru had been robbed of his cattle.

OCTOBER

It is a curious thing; you kicking inside my belly. It does ask
questions about a creator.

When I am out in the bush hunting, I sometimes have to
leave the hunting party for a moment and wander off to find a
suitable place far enough away to "punguza chai" as it is
called in Swahili (bring down the tea level). I bring my gun,
since it is in the most unsuspecting situations dangerous
things can happen. Often, the surrounding landscape is dry.
It's hot, and the sun sucks on earth, gradually shrinking it like
a boiled sweet, until the rains arrive again. I wonder what
might grow from the local rain I produce on that very spot.
Something will. It takes so very little. The plant growing
there, could it think, would probably tell the world that there
was a God. Why otherwise did it get life, when everything
else about it, its entire universe, in fact, lay quite lifeless?
Somebody arrived and gave it, specifically it, life. Arrived
exactly there, from the heavens above it and breathed life into
it, just like that. To that straw of grass, I might be God.

But even if it is so, one god must be the creation of
another, in an infinitely long line, unless I allow for the
existence of randomness somewhere. For who, if not
randomness, made me go just there and not to the other bush
just beside it? Was that seed that grew from my piss a chosen
seed? If there was a meaning with bringing that seed into
existence, it was a meaning I never designed or even
fathomed. You see, I ignorantly just needed to have a pee. If
there was a purpose to the special arrival of that straw of
grass, I was merely the puppet of a greater god, who made me
go to that exact spot. And so as a god I am merely the

creation of another god all the way up into a quite invisible spot in eternity. One god fathering the next, one god mothering the next again, until enter the stage, the mother of all reason, the father of all reason; Randomness!

Also, little has to do with me or you, though it often really seems so.

I was on my way to a particular spot in a huge hunting area when I met a giraffe walking down the track I was driving on. Though I drove up behind it, it did not take that one step to the right or to the left off the road, but started running forward on it instead. To the giraffe, it must have seemed like I was following it. I was, of course, not in the slightest interested in the giraffe, but in getting to my destination. I tried everything: To stop the car completely for a long while. This resulted in the giraffe standing in the middle of the road staring at me in that inexhaustible way only giraffes can. I tried going off the road to get around it. I slowed down to give it time to walk off. When I tried speeding up behind it, the giraffe just kept running ahead of my car and getting increasingly panicked, its legs comically flailing in all directions.

In the end, more from taking a wrong step, it veered off and fretfully galloped off to the side. It must have been with a heart pumping fearfully that it stopped further away, half hidden behind an acacia, and stared at its pursuer. In the giraffe's mind, I had been chasing it and it had got away from me in the nick of time.

One discovers, having been upset about other people, that most things that happen to or around you are not about you. You just happened to be there.

Mostly, when I think about religion, however, I do not think of sprouting plants and giraffes. I think about how much I dislike missionaries, still so plentiful here in Africa. The bible dealers pimping for clients to make hooked on their sugar.

Despite all of this, don't ask me to renounce the divine in other forms. I will not be clear on the subject. I call myself an agnostic, but really I am more of a fair-weather friend to the school of the agnostic, while making pacts and deals with divinities when I am fearful or hopeful or depressed enough.

Once, I had tea with a splendid cardinal in a restaurant in Bangui in the Central African Republic, after having spent a month with some pygmies in the forest. While I watched the Congo River flow by, I asked him if he never had doubts about what missionaries had done to African tribes like the pygmies. He answered me he did not need to doubt about anything his church had done in Africa. "In fact," he told me, "the catholic church does not doubt."

And so we just drank each our cup of tea silently and I could not look him in the eyes any longer. Instead, I kept looking at the Congo River flowing by and thought about all the bridges that could be built by doubt.

A shame it was, for his eyes as his face were very interesting and I imagine we could have spoken about many things for a long time.

A shame it possibly was too, for the pygmies.

OCTOBER

I wince when I realise that you too will be dealt your share of pain and conflict. I hope that only very little of it is to do with how I was as a mother.

We are plodding about in the same place, I have just known it longer than you. Not that I understand much about life. I imagine knowing life is much like knowing a person; what you absolutely know about them one moment changes significantly the next.

I never saw the point of trying to hide from pain and conflict, but I know that there are ways. Some people prefer to lie on the ground and play dead, others take up rowdy company permanently: drugs, alcohol, and other noises. By all means, I spend my share of extravagant hours with that lot. I know them all very well - they dress up splendidly. The trick is to keep them on the level of acquaintanceships. They are entertaining, so let them entertain you, never entertain them. They are like an evolutionary flaw, where the parasite wants to kill the host.

When, one of these days, you are hit square on by a great pain; it is like bumping into a lion. Don't turn your back on it and run. Running releases its killer instinct. Rest assured, your mother knows that you can never outrun a lion. Instead, keep an eye on it, without staring. Carefully distance yourself with very slow and measured movements, but keep facing in its direction while carefully taking in what is happening around you.

I have always let all of my emotions range free, except for self-pity. Self-pity is another word for stagnation (small, evaporating, pea green ponds, with no water-flow, spring to mind). Pity is bad enough. No one deserves pity, but self-pity will mix into your blood like an astringent. Once your veins are pumping self-pity around, you will become alien to your own core truth and start making up strange reasons to stay unchanged, while getting more and more sick in your relationship with yourself. That is a bit like having one of those bizarre allergies people can have towards their own hair or skin. Infected with self-pity, you will start scratching and tearing at yourself, until you have quite torn yourself apart.

NOVEMBER

Last night I dreamt of a strange sort of machine. I had to walk through many swamps to get to it and almost disappeared under the green of the surfaces several times. I saw other people walking far away. They were going in the same direction as I was, but they had taken another road. They looked at me and I looked at them, none of us surprised about at what the other was doing. The road they were on was dry, and I could see the light playing on their black patent leather shoes. They brushed their trousers to rid themselves of red dust. I reflected on why I had so foolishly chosen to cross the swamps instead of taking the road. Finally, the swamp ended. The ground hardened under my feet, and my legs felt light again. I moved forward calmly, knowing where I was going. I walked into a house and was first shown to a small table where I could make myself a cup of tea and was then told to go to the bookkeeper. Having looked for the bookkeeper for a long time, I finally found him in a rectangular white room. He was sitting on a tall chair with his back leaning against the wall and a pencil and ledger on his lap, obviously waiting. Not for me specifically. He was more like a museum guard waiting for the first visitor of the day.

The machine that I now saw sitting in the middle of the room was called the "machine of all possibilities of truth." It was a huge, empty concrete box, about two metres tall and eight metres long. It was closed on all sides except for two small windows on the top, placed about two metres apart. Later, I noticed that there must be a door on the side of the box where the bookkeeper sat. To look into one of the small windows (you could only look at one at a time) you had to take two steps up on a small wooden ladder put in front of each end of the box. As I took the two steps up, I noticed that another person, I don't know if it was a woman or a man, had climbed the ladder on the other side of the box. Now this person stood looking through the other window.

As soon as we were both in "our place" the bookkeeper got off his chair and I could hear how he opened a small door in the concrete box. I understood that he had gone inside to place something for us to see through the small windows. When he came out again, he climbed his chair once more and opened his ledger, pen ready.

I realised that he was blind.

"You first," he said, turning his face towards me. I looked through the window and described what I saw. I used words like "black", "hairy". But I could not make out what I was looking at as a whole and complained about that. The bookkeeper, who had meticulously noted down everything I said about the object, then turned to the other visitor. He used many words to describe what he saw at his end, though some of them might have been the same as mine. I complained again that we could not see the whole object and therefore could not possibly give him a proper description of what was in the box. To this he said to me;

"Don't you understand that this is the machine of all possibilities of truth? Only like this can we ever get closer to the essence of actual seeing. By taking away all recognition of an object as a whole, you and thousands of other people can give us fragments of a description of something until we can build a truth devoid of subjectivity. If you see the whole object, the truth you give me will be tainted by your memories and your experience. I just need to know what is in the box and not who you are and what your history is."

It is tempting to insist that what you see so clearly is the truth. But then sometimes, there is an opening, a possibility, a glimpse of something else. Looking through a crack, you might discover that to another world, there under the surface of earth's crust, the roots are the crown of the tree.

NOVEMBER

Nairobi, Kenya

I am in Nairobi waiting. Your arrival is to be called in a short while. There are no decent hospitals in Tanzania, so your father and I have come up here.

The time table is clear.

I have started waiting for you. They say you are almost here. I go to the hospital, the place of arrival. Wait on the platform. Pace the nights there. Drum the skin on my stomach. It is tight as a tick. I Can't sleep anymore. Can't lie down. Rest is when I doze off in a sitting position. The loud

speaker says there are delays. I wait some more. Feel
impatient now. Irritated. Had enough of this waiting game.
The entire world here, in this hospital, this station, is smiling
because they are waiting for some new passenger to arrive, or
crying because they are saying goodbye.

Then, there it is.

First a speck, then bigger and bigger and expanding, until
it arrives right here. The train has come, grinds to a halt with
a screeching sound.

Doors fly open. People pour all around me, as if they all
know where they are heading. I am immobile in the human
flow around me. They push me this way and that. I no longer
have control over my body. Before a mist falls down over us
and I lose consciousness, I see people rush back and forth,
carry things in and out of the revolving double doors. Then
all disappears for some time.

The mist lifts slowly. The world appears again. I can make out
the solid mass of bodies and commotion, I do not know for
how long I was cut off and what has happened while my eyes
were closed.

I look for you in the commotion of humans. I fear a little. I
can't move. There are faces everywhere. Faces I don't know.
They take up too much of my field of vision. I can't look
down properly. I can't tell one voice from another. Maybe you
are not there. Panic tightens its grip over my collarbones.
Maybe you were afraid to arrive here.

I want to get up and come to you. Find you. Help you find
me, but I can't. I have to wait here, numbed, held into place
by the moving masses. "Watch out!" I want to shout. So much

that can happen to you before you find me. You are so small. I know how easily small things are lost in crowds. But there is a static over my voice as if someone has nudged my radio frequency dial, just enough to shift its clarity.

Then things calm down a bit. The voices of the masses trail off as they leave.

Finally, it is just you and me here.

I see your hands first, the arms stretch out, but the fists are clenched. Then I see feet with no shoes. I only know that it is you, when I see your face turned up towards mine, undoubting. I take a deep sigh of relief and exhaustion. How did you know to come to me? Did really nobody step on those minute naked toes coming over here? How is that possible?

I don't understand it all and I am overtaken with humble faith in this apparition that you seem to be.

You take my hand firmly and want us to leave. I get up and obey and know I shall keep walking to wherever you will take me, forever. You are naked and have no luggage and I wonder if anything I have will fit you, but you ask for nothing like that.

"Open your heart," you communicate to me sharply, "shift over everything else," is what you let me understand. You are moving in for good, you explain, quite matter-of-factly.

They cut me open to lift you out. Then they stitched me up and sent us on our way.

I know one thing, however, for I feel it clearly; something of yours was left behind in my innermost body.

YEAR ONE

JANUARY

Oldonyo sambu, Tanzania

You are here.

People keep asking me the same thing when I present them to you for the first time. They say: "Isn't it the most amazing thing? Isn't it a surprise that this love for your child is so gigantic? Don't you find you are shocked or scared of this massive emotion that you are suddenly capable of?"

When they have finished speaking, they look at me, to check if I am feeling what I am supposed to. To see if I am feeling how a mother should. For years and years, I lived all on my own, isolated and to myself up here. I lived what they think is the hard-arsed life of having a gun on your shoulder or a sharpened pen in your hand. A life of ammo belts with bullets, as opposed to baby legs, wrapped around my hips.

And when I was not doing that, I sat up here amongst my books and wrote. I had lovers much younger than myself, that I mercilessly kept out of reach of my intimate life for the last eight years, before I met your father. As they imagine it, I might just be a little cold, incapable of such emotion. You never know is what their eyes say when they search for how I react to their words.

I might nod finally, for I don't want to get in to this discussion with any of them, but most of the time I show no signs of what I am thinking and don't comment.

No, I don't feel frightened or surprised by the onset of feelings I have for you. I was never astonished or bawled over at my vulnerability, my complete capacity to feel boundlessly. In my entire life, I never saw a single more commanding thing than love, nor anything that even compares to its ability to inflate in me.

I was born with a space carved out for you already. Now you have at last stepped in to take the place that was always rightfully and naturally yours, and nothing in the world feels less surprising. Things have come right. You have always been there, as the weather has always been there, and I am so much smaller, so in the mercy of such great things, that I am forced to take both of your arrival for granted.

Yes, there are many moments when my entire being swells looking at you, but the awe, the gratefulness I feel so deeply is not towards my ability to love, rather it is towards nature having made me your mother.

FEBRUARY

Yesterday, we drove down from our hill and into Arusha town. You half-sleeping in your infant car seat, I half-sleeping in my big car seat. I had been sitting up most of the night, half-sleeping, you at my breast, half-sleeping. Every time you nodded off, my nipple slipped out of your mouth and you started crying as loudly as a siren full alarm. As if you were the sole guardian of the last hold of mother's milk, and having slept on your guard was now awake and ready to fight. Your father is in Sweden. He will be back in a couple of days, I think.

The dirt track off the farm and onto the main Namanga Road runs between the buttock shaped foothills of Mount Meru. We drive on the erosion, and there is a particular place we pass through, where the hills on either side of the road rise steeply. Here we are erased in clouds of dust and for a moment you can hardly see what is us and our car, and what are herds of cattle and goats or the Waarusha goading them forward. All of us - car, goats, dust, herdsmen - inch forward at the same slow speed, intertwined, like molasses sliding downwards. Often we have to stop for a few minutes to avoid driving into a crevasse.

We are on our way to the fruit and vegetable market in Arusha. I am not looking forward to the eternal arguments I will have to have again with the women there. They will go on until I get the same price as the black customer who preceded me. On the market they call out "mzungu, mzungu," "whitey". Though it is not meant maliciously. It is just stating the obvious, like saying, "Look! It is raining." A reminder of my place in society. I hear myself saying in Swahili: "Why do you comment on the colour of my skin? The colour of our blood is the same. I speak Swahili as well as you do. I have lived here longer than anywhere else. Maybe I lived here before you were born. This is my home. Why do you give me a different price for your tomatoes than you just did to the customer before me?"

Then they laugh delightedly and give me the tomatoes at a normal price and compliment me on my Swahili and keep laughing so much that I laugh too. I wish we could skip to that part immediately.

MARCH

Something just frightened you a moment ago. I am not sure what it was, but you cried. I held you close and walked around with your little face lodged close to my neck. When I put you down, you held on to two of my fingers tightly, as if you were afraid of sleep stealing you away from me. Of course, sleep always does. Now that you have gone there, your face is looking blissful and a small smile is forming on your lips.

Fear is that dark creature you don't recognise, that moves when you move, that gets smaller the closer you get to it and bigger the further you step away.

I remember when I had to follow a wounded buffalo on my own the first time. I must have been about 25 years old. We were in an area quite far south in Tanzania and it was the second client or hunting-guest I had booked. I had spun stories about my vast experience to the nice enough fair haired middle-aged American, and he arrived with a broad smile and a big gun.

It had been a catch-22 situation to get started as a professional hunter. I had been an apprentice for several years, longer than most, to good hunters. Also, I had spent time in Northern Kenya culling zebras and hunting the odd buffalo on weekends.

Still, apprentices are never left alone with a wounded buffalo. To get clients to go hunting buffalo with you, you had to have a certain amount of experience, but you could not get the experience without that first client. The other young professional hunters were given their first hunts by some kind older hunter, but not I. I was the only girl in the business. No one would take a chance on the girl. The only way to break it was to jump into the deep end. Here, it meant to lie full throttle and hope someone interested enough in hunting a buffalo in Tanzania for a good price would be inexperienced enough, or merciful enough, to ignore the loose ends in your tale.

Alas, I found and booked my blue-eyed ticket. Only after I had already booked him did I go looking for the hunting company that would have me and sold it to them. I was hoping the area descriptions I had given to the guest would seem reasonably compatible to where we ended up going to. I put all my trust in a combination of his lack of experience and my ability to learn fast.

The client shot a very old bull late in the afternoon. It immediately turned and disappeared into dense shrubbery before any of us could see where it had been hit. There was nothing I could do but wait until the next morning. Inside such a thick bush, at this time of day, it would have been impossible to see anything. It would be completely dark soon. For a while we stood and listened, but it was quiet. By the time we got back to the car, it was pitch black. The hunting guest was quiet out of worry, and I was already beginning to feel the sticky fear rise in my neck. I joked with him during the hour it took to drive back to camp, while the cold soup in my stomach made me sick.

We skipped drinks and had our showers. Two of the men brought buckets of hot water. As they passed my open tent-door, they offered me their big smiles and said the usual respectful greetings. I heard them climb the ladder and pour the water in, while chatting about something I did not hear or listen to. They were lucky to have the job of heating water, I thought. The calm of just putting a few logs under the big drums of water, light it in the afternoon and then just get ready to haul a few buckets over to my tent at 7:30, or when they heard me come into camp. Maybe they drank milky cups of tea while waiting. I guess I got a better bed than they. Mine was almost like the guest's bed, for that they trusted me to do my part perfectly, poor sods. The dinner conversation was strained and kept circling about how bad he felt about the prospects of having wounded a buffalo. Like most other people, he only spoke about the pain the animal must be in and avoided mentioning the part that was disturbing his sense of pride. Again and again he asked me: "Do you think it's dead?" I kept telling him I thought it was and that we would go straight out and find it early the next morning, and if not, that I would sort it out, so "not to worry". I sounded awfully sure of myself, noticed how I even managed a smirk and a comment about loving the challenge, while the blood sunk from my head towards my feet like water to oil. None of us had any doubts that the animal was wounded and very much alive.

Straight after dinner, we said goodnight and took each our path towards our tents. I sat on the ground outside mine for a few minutes while brushing my teeth. The sound of the brush was hollow, the light of the moon hard, making everything look solid. It was with a steady resolve that I told myself I would die the next day. It was almost a relief to try to just accept this black thing that had been trying to get into my heart for several hours now. I knew my level of experience with wounded buffalo was insignificant. I also knew I would not run. I think I even spoke to the moon, whispered something with a tongue that felt swollen from dryness, perfectly aware that the moon did not have a penny for my thoughts. This night was the one of last farewells and I took them.

There were a few fits of sleep, but mostly I lay awake. The sound of a scops owl nearby, and the shrill bark of a jackal, kept me company for most of the dark hours. I kept seeing different scenarios of how I would die the next day. I knew I would not bring the client with me all the way into the thickets. This was my mess. Nothing to do with a poor sod who had paid to go hunting with someone who had never followed a wounded buffalo on her own before. What I saw clearest was the toss. When the buffalo lowered its head, cocking it to one side. My shuffling steps, my shot, that was far too slow and missed the brain, the sound of breaking branches. Then finally, how it hooked me and whipped me up in the air with a quick jerk. I had seen what it looked like, had noted and compared at all the bullfights I had watched in Spain. Sometimes, in my midnight filmshow, the bull would turn back again and finish me off. In other scenarios, it kept running while the blood drained out of me. The buffalo running away was a testament to my inability to do my job, my foolhardiness and arrogance for everyone to witness. The consequences for someone else to clean up. That "someone else" would be one of those hunters who had always said, had known, from the very beginning, that I could never have a hunting life in the bush. Who had known that following wounded buffalos was for men with legs widely planted on the ground and big dry hands that gripped the gun, making it look lighter in their grip than I ever could. One of those hunters who had doubled up laughing when I told them I did what they did for a living. They would be right and I would be dead. By this stage, the fear of dying was taken over by the familiar knot in my stomach when I imagined how they laughed behind my back.

A moment later, a new death scenario would come washing in from some hitherto unknown place, and the whole thing started all over again. The idea of death was no longer as pure as I had imagined it before. In my first youth, safely tucked in bed in my childhood home, I had imagined death to be a clean matter of the soul. Now I merely felt nausea and cold sweat at the thought of limp flesh. Death would rob my body of emotion and make it meaningless. The dead human body, void of the wise-looking beauty of other still bodies like trees, has no beauty without motion. The still meat of man is dumb. It made me want to vomit.

I saw my mother and my father before me, crushed. Heads bent. My tall father's face, even more hollow than before. My mother's scream, then her eyes darting wildly and hands flailing like creatures trying to cut loose and run away for good. When I rose the next morning, my calm had nothing to do with bravery. I was numbed by hours of unrest, hours of fear. The escape that acceptance finally offers is what the brain succumbs to when it can produce no more images of what it deems unavoidable.

I went to breakfast with the guest, clear-headed and freed from emotion. I ate my scrambled eggs and asked myself if they would still be yellow when my stomach was opened up by a buffalo's horn in a couple of hours. The client spoke a lot, and I nodded and didn't hear a word he was saying.

It did not take as long as I remembered to get back to the place we had left the previous night. I switched off the engine, got out of the car, grabbed my gun and told the guest I would be back as soon as I found it. He only stayed behind reluctantly, but I gave him no choice. I don't know if the idea of shame or that of guilt would have been larger for me, if he had come with me that day and something would have happened to him. It was something I was not prepared to take with me into the thick of those bushes.

I remember how I stood a couple of metres, still in the clearing, before the quiet clump of bright green, dense foliage, and looked at the ground for drops of blood. Suddenly, I realised something of great relief. It was the sum of the situation that was frightening, not the individual steps. The steps were in themselves too small to carry something too bad for me to handle.

I lifted a branch and took one first step into the thicket. One foot in front of the other, as slowly as I wanted to. I had the entire day. I could stop in my tracks and listen for as long as I wanted. By each step, where the buffalo still had not come charging out of the bushes, my heart strengthened a little. I learned that danger could not show itself entirely in one step. This way, it became impossible to feel the entirety of your imaginary outcomes. It was about bringing second by second reality close while merely concentrating on listening to the crack of a branch. I learned that massive fear can be broken down into step size portions.

When I finally found the buffalo, it was stone cold dead. During my absolutely worst night of fear until then, the buffalo had just been quietly cooling in the dark.

Only later did I meet my first charging buffalo.

APRIL

Lately, thoughts have woken me up at night. It appears most people around me live by a magic formula that gives them more peace than I have. I am not sure if they are just acting, but they seem more at ease with life. I hope I can bring you peace. Growing up, I had passionate love around me, but little peace. I don't want you to always be thrown about in waves of emotion.

My only constant company is an enormous, violently handsome hound: passion. I share everything I have with it. Nature, my books, friends, my birth family, my lover, you, I eat with passion. At any cost, at any consequence, down to the last morsel, wool in my pockets, blood in my veins, I share what I have with this dog. Keep nothing to myself. I don't know how to do anything else. I never have. It is a striking sight when we walk through town together, passion and I. We are a handsome couple, me and this wild creature strolling next to me willingly. I take it with me everywhere, this creature with its godlike strength and its slobbering beastly jaws. Its enormous face at my side it licks and bites, eats out of my hand or shits by my feet.

Yet, as time passes, I understand that I don't own this capricious dog. I am its obedient companion, the fortunate ignoramus shining in the light of its grace, not the other way around. I can only hope that it will not be noticed by anyone that I am the fool, completely and utterly at its beck and call.

Judging from what I see in those fiercely shining little eyes, I suspect you will take the lead from of this creature from me. By then I hope I can teach you how to make this stubborn old hound obey "sit".

MAY

Much harder to control is time. There is nothing you can do to reason with time. Time eats up everything. Literally all disappears down its gullet. When I was a in my late teens, I was afraid that time would clean swallow my life before I could grab hold of it properly. Look straight at the hard face of time. Don't turn away from it. Because those who are afraid enough of its horror create, explore, think, study, feel, love and do things others haven't done before. If you are aware of the insatiable hunger of time, you will fight for what you want without fear of most things. Nothing will stop those who are more afraid of time than anything else.

Right now, I feel like a rock that sits in a river and lets time divide and pass me on both sides. One day eats the other and I seem to always be one step behind it, in some kind of soul-jet-lag where I am sleepwalking during the day and half lucid during the night. In the dark with wide-open eyes, but seeing nothing. My emotions shift erratically and there is never enough permanence to regain balance. I seem drunk to myself. One moment I have lost all foothold, the next I lose so much foothold again that I understand in hindsight that I must have regained some in between. It is not your fault, nor is it mine. I gave you life. For that you plugged me into eternity and that is so much bigger than I, and is making so much more noise than I can withstand, that I have absolved in to it for a moment. That is all.

Last night I held you in my arms all night. It is cold outside. Up here at about 2000 metres, it gets freezing in June. Especially behind tent walls. You have your first flu. I am not worried, but you were. I know it will pass soon. A little fever and a clogged nose, shiny eyes peeping out from under a thick duvet. We hardly slept at all last night. You cried, and I sang. It is the time now, as it is every seven years, for the young skolios with their white panted faces and feathers, to be transformed into warriors. Your crying only seized every time a group of fiercely shouting and chanting skolios went by in the dark. At first light, you fell fast asleep. Then I went downstairs and made tea. I thought to myself that I wished I could take a night like yesterday, where we hovered together in a bubble of misery and trust, and keep it on a thin chain around my neck, for I know things like that are often lost. That time has them for breakfast.

At least there is something eternal about making tea. I imagine that when you grow up, tea will still be boiling water and a spoonful of leaves for each cup and one for the pot.

JUNE

Nature here, as you are beginning to notice, is a grand myriad of colours, shapes. They are so different from those that I first encountered in life.

Where I grew up, nature is better described with words like "pretty", "beautiful" maybe. Our forest had not a single thorn in it, but soft, broad leaves that rustled obediently and bent to the wind. When the rain fell on our land in Sweden, the petrichor was mild, pleasant, the scent of a lenient soil opening gently to the habitual touch of soft rain.

Here, the cataclysmic torrents peel the earth, rip away the top layer of soil and then pound the ground, until it cracks open and pushes life as if it is spitting it out.

I did not fathom what you will know of slender acacias sticking out of the ground like spears, housing ants and whistling when the dust devils push through their spiky pods. Yearly fires didn't sweep the forest of my childhood, leaving that stinging smell of singed and desperately incinerated ground. A smell that I sometimes miss now.

The undisputed monarch of the landscape of my childhood was your babu. His intimidating roar was unmistakable, as was his vast knowledge about every inch of the animal kingdom on earth. It perplexed him why not everyone could identify a bird from half a mile away, since its outline and flight pattern were so distinctive. If the bird flying overhead was edible, it was hard for him to understand where in the difficulty might lie in picking it from the sky with a shotgun. His long legs strode, they never walked. My sister and I had to run to keep up, like jackals. When he stopped, he either shouted at us or tangoed with us. He never left the house to go to a dinner party without first having climbed up on the long kitchen table for us. He looked at us with a mad stare and combed his hair forward over his forehead. Chatting and shouting, he hobbled up and down the kitchen table in his black patent leather shoes, imitating a chimpanzee, until my mother came down to our laughter a while later.

The others — people who came who were neither close friends nor people who understood our kingdom — I didn't really notice. Our world was one where humans were less significant. We spoke much more about conservation, hunting and catching fish, than of the humans outside our lands. The forest, the archipelago, the deer, the vicent, the wild boar, all the different birds. Our forest was closed to the public, and the villages outside never quite forgave the three generations of my family for caring more about the forest, the animals and the sea, than humans. It seemed to them gruesome, incomprehensible, and suspicious. It apparently seemed like a convoluted disrespect towards them. As far back as your great grandfather, they made sure that we understood they felt this way. To me, it was as if they were on the other side of the glass. I never doubted that we were looking in to a cage and they were looking out.

Your babu lived for the animals and the forest, like his father did and for a 100 years they spoke loudly and clearly about what they thought about mans behaviour in nature. They kicked up some dust in the human flock.

Here in Oldonyo sambu, the Mwaarusha cattle kick up the dust that settles on our things. We watch the land erode a little more each year. Everything erodes. Changes. Maybe this is every generation's sadness by default — the mourning that sets in after having seen enough transformation, wear and tear.

We go for a walk in the late afternoon and talk to the Mwaarusha, to see if there is a cow that will let you kiss it while a Mwaarusha herds boy holds it by the horns for you. We watch the women and girls walking up to the mountain, pangas balancing on their heads, to get firewood in an ever shrinking forest. They chatter and laugh and shout to me they want to have you in exchange for one of their children or for two cows. I laugh and shout: "Next Monday, but it is ten cows," and I wonder each time what life has brought us before next Monday.

JULY

It is winter in Tanzania now. Up here it is cold and I wrap you in blankets until you shout at me wordlessly to take some of them off.

Your father got back late last night. When we woke up this morning, a pigeon was sitting cooped up on the bedside table, inches away from my pillow. It must have had sat there the entire night. It made me feel we were witnessing a miracle. A miracle I wanted to smile at with your father, but maybe he sees miracles in other places. I wish he would tell me where he sees miracles. Surely, he sees them somewhere with his brown eyes.

If I was a child again and back where I grew up, I would imagine that the cherry trees were flowering out at the lily croft, our little hut on the other side of the bay.

One produced black cherries, one produced red, and then there was the one that produced yellow cherries. I liked the red the best, and somehow presumed that my mother liked the yellow best and that my father liked the black ones. Then, with a belly full, I would walk out onto the wooden bridge and dive into the cold water. I think you can only really enjoy standing on a bottom of brackish water—where your feet sink in to the soft, black mud — and only adore the slight tingle of swimming along reeds hiding giant pike, if you have done it ever since the beginning of your life. The semisweet water of the Blekinge archipelago, so mild and muddy compared to the clear and salty waves on Zanzibar or Mafia Island, that you may get to know so well, is mine. I will take you to a place by the Indian Ocean, repeat an experience there for you enough times, so that something by the sea becomes yours too.

Owning land on paper has nothing to do with what is really ours. We own the land our senses know.

When I drove up here the first time, I noticed in the distance a big acacia tortilis on a ridge coming off Mount Meru. I said to myself: "When that tree falls, I will move."

The other day, coming back from Arusha, I noticed it had
fallen. It was lying on its side up there in the middle of the
green grass, tilted like an umbrella drying in the sun.

So, we must go soon. I realise too that we are very far away
from a school.

We must find places that can be all yours. We must plant
our feet in fresh soil and I can't wait to watch you, us, grow
there. For nothing on earth will make me feel richer than
watching you grow next to me, my little love, and the soil
around your feet must be something quite special. Something
rich, especially chosen to let you root.

I think we will burn this house down as soon as we have
found our new place. Yes, why not? That is what we will do. It
will not be an act of violence to burn this house down, it will
not be an attempt to forget something. My years here have
been some of the most important of my life and I don't wish
to forget a single one of them. When we roll down the hill
and look up here one last time, we will see a happy piece of
our lives rooted there, together with the little forest we have
created. A forest that can keep growing in peace without us
disturbing it any more. Safaris just end, so others can begin.

Yes, what a good idea. I shall invite people for dry martinis
and dinner on the lawn, and then we will watch it burn.

JULY

Mwanya, (*gap-tooth-beauty*, as it means in Swahili), today I
was about to put Laito on the bus and send him home to his
village outside Kondoa. The plan, and it was his own
suggestion, was that he go back to the village where a big part
of his father's family is from. Here he will try to find a suitable

lady of his tribe who would like to come back with him and take the job of being your yaya. Laito and I have drawn up a list of criteria together. In order of importance.

1. Must be kind.

2. Must love children and have at least one of her own.

3. Her child or children are grown and the opportunity to work somewhere else is an exciting prospect.

4. Must have a sense of humour.

5. Must know Swahili (as opposed to only her tribal language). No need to know English.

6. Must know how to use a bow and arrow, like indeed women of his tribe do, and will want to teach our little girl how to use one from an early age. Also can show her how to track little animals in the garden and show which plants are edible and explain tell what the animals are saying to each other and her.

But then suddenly she arrived, Bahati. Taller than any other woman I had even seen, with a firm handshake and bundles of colourful kangas wrapped around her head and her more than generous hips. She knows nothing about arrows and tracking, and laughed loudly and looked at me curiously when I asked her. She then pointed towards Laito, who is half of her size, and freely asked if he could not take care of such things. He nodded.

She sang to you immediately and if indeed there was such a thing as fate; it was in that song. We had not spoken of salaries and such things, but I asked Laito to not get on that bus.

When I was little, we used to go to my maternal grandmother's summer house on the Danish coast by the Baltic sea. I sometimes wonder how I am going to give you summers as beautiful as those. My mother would put parsley in our hair and tell us many tales. There was singing. The selection wasn't vast, and that is why I remember the words of each song with clarity. We did not sing the same songs at home as we did in your great grandmother's summer house.

There were winter songs and summer songs.

Two songs were sung by all the children. One was about bees and the other was about the nest of a lark hidden on the heath, in danger of being discovered by the evils of boys and foxes. The song about the bee, is one of the main theme tunes to my memories of that time of my life. It is a song that lies safely in an unbreakable glass case, amongst other beautiful and harsh memories that stuck to me during my early years. Imprints impossible to change, now that the door to childhood has been closed.

When Bahati walked into our little home in Oldonyo Sambu and sang the song about the bee, but in Swahili, nothing could have persuaded me to turn her away. Without no more ado, she then told me: "My baby will not wear a white shirt that has not been washed better," and, "my baby will have her own basin for baths."

So the world spun fast suddenly and Bahati hurled into our lives, never followed by a shadow of doubt.

AUGUST.

A page for you to keep for later.

Shh, don't cry for too long.

It does not matter what it is. You left your lover, or your lover left you, or you feel smaller than a speck floating by in the light. Whatever it might be this time, still yourself. If I am yet here, ring me, come to me immediately. I will put down what is in my hands and listen. If I am not, just trust what I say to you now. It will go away. It will get better. This too shall pass. NO! Don't protest. Listen to your mother. It will get better. If you want it to.

Close your eyes. Can you feel my shawl wrapped around your back and chest? My mother gave me a shawl, and I give you one too. Wrap it all the way around, twice, put your face inside it.

Is it awfully silent and lonely where you are? Is that what you are saying? You can always imagine that I am quartering you to one side, in the blind spot, though it is not quite like that. No, that is not such a poor picture. You know when you see something at the corner of your eye that disappears when you try to look at it directly. Still, you will have seen it. If I have died by now, or when I do, then I will not slip into the next room, like Henry Scott-Hollands poem says. I don't believe it is like that. It is a foolish thought.

You were made from my blood, however. I am some of the notes in the beat of your pulse. Listen. Can you hear me drumming steadily from inside? You see, I did lie about one thing: It is not the sea you can hear inside that conch. It is the flow of our blood. Find a conch now and put it on your bedside table. In the dark, take it to your ear, listen to us. Then rest.

SEPTEMBER

You are ten months old now. Just before you turn eleven months, I will go hunting again. Since I was six months pregnant with you, I started worrying about being away from you for three weeks before your first birthday.

"Don't worry," they say, "your father will be here." Yes, I know he is a father who loves you and that you will be in safe hands. It is just that I am your mother. I don't care what the scientists say about this and that. I am your mother. You came from my body. They cut me open and pulled you out and closed me up again, thinking that was that and that I am me exactly as I was be before. It is true, I am perfectly stitched up and healed now, but they didn't see that you pushed something into the gap between two of my ribs as you kicked off. I like this invisible treasure you left behind, but it also brings some madness, for it seems to want to get back to you. The further I move away from you, the more it rips and tugs.

People tell me I will miss you, more than you will miss me. I hope so. I already know that the nights will be the worst.

I am worried. Not so worried that I will call it off, but I am anxious. I hope you will sleep well, play well, eat well. And I think of your babu, my father, he will have an operation while I am gone.

SEPTEMBER

I just received information from the head office. The area in western Tanzania that I am going to is so full of elephant poachers now that things are getting out of hand.

Slaughtered herds of ten and fifteen elephants were found by two of the other professional hunters. Grim axed holes in their heads, where the ivory has been removed, the rest left to rot. The poachers are not afraid of the likes of us. They just shoot anything that get's in their tunnel vision. We pose a threat to them by just being there and that puts a spanner in their works, but here is not much we can physically do to stop these new mad gangs. The government will not let us arm our antipoaching teams. We have them there, ready to go. I am ready to get involved too, but how much can we do on the ground? Throw rocks at AK47's? One of my colleagues was killed by such a raging gang, by a shot to the head, not so long ago.

Already, I have stayed up at night, while you slept through the pre-rain storms that rattle our little hut, thinking of ways to do something about it. China still, like a hundred years ago, has their insatiable hunger for Ivory.

I think of my father suddenly. A pang of worry turns my stomach. I think of the operation he will go through while I am away. But we all know that he is strong, stubborn as well. He has told me he is going hunting in a few weeks. This will take him through.

The pre-rain drought has arrived in our little home, on the top of the hill. It is getting difficult to see the rim of the Ngorongoro crater. Dust devils swipe across the plains below and our war-loving neighbours, the Waarusha, have taken up their spears to fight with the Maasai about the cattle they habitually steal from each other. Fatal amounts of blood rarely drained, but it happens. If we had owned a single cow, both tribes would consider me the biggest thief of all. God gave cattle to the Masai and the Waarusha, anyone else who owns any, clearly stole it from them at some stage.

Birds of all sizes come to us, from all directions. They land bravely, just a few feet away, and venture to drink in the little birdbath outside. Your first proper word is "ndege," Swahili for bird. Most of the birds coming past us are en route to other places.

When the summer air began to cool, the light slowly greying, geese started congregating in the hundreds on the fields by my childhood home. We could hear them as they came in from all sides. They landed in clusters somewhere near and waited for more to arrive. Then one day, as on cue, they all broke for the skies together. Lifted like a veil caught by the wind. My father would open the windows in our parent's bedroom and call up to them. Like a man calling to his god. And the geese responded by turning sharply, circling our home once more, in the hundreds, before returning to their set course to cross the world. Here in Oldonyo sambu, when you have your morning nap, crows and white-naped ravens, jealous of their own image in the glass, fly against the window. They peck at the glass, sweep the windows with their black cape-like wings and wake you up. When the birds have so rudely interfered and Bahati needs to go outside in the harsh of midday to hang the washing, she comes down to me and leaves you here, in my writing tent, to crawl around and discover your first world.

She says that there is too much dust out there for you this month, that the sun is too scorching, that the grass by the washing line has become too spiky for you to crawl around

in, that the wind blows too hard. She is right. We are here
inside my office tent together.

SEPTEMBER

For as long as possible, I want you to be inside this little tent
with me. Let the harshness of dust and white light and
mad-eyed elephant poachers come later. We will pull down
the zip and lay down quietly on the chaise longue for an hour.
Let us watch the shadows of the leaves play on the pale
canvas, like you have always loved to do, since your eyes first
opened and you thought to look up.

Just for five more minutes, ten more minutes. Just for a
moment of ever. You and I and the silhouettes of leaves on
canvas, nothing else.

SEPTEMBER

**On a small plane bound for the bush airstrip in our
Rungwa hunting block, western Tanzania.**
I packed my bags with trepidation. My stomach clenched at
the idea of danger. I arrived at Arusha's small local airport
and realised that I would be gone for three weeks from you.
Your father drove me down. He did not empathise with my
worry about leaving you.

I will soon be in an area full of elephant poachers. They
have told me that in this area, that I had always loved, I could
no longer go hunting on foot for 21 days, like I love doing. It
is too dangerous now. Instead, I have had to change the safari
the last minute, to a more "normal safari" where you walk

when you are hunting, but use the car to take you from A to B.

I felt so lonely at the airport that I started talking to a woman who is an acquaintance from Kenya. A woman who has neither liked me, nor ever been very kind to me, but whom I knew was a mother. I asked her if she thought you would be all right for so long without me and she assured me you would. It did not help, and I felt foolish when I walked away from her. I had wanted your father to calm me.

I met up with the hunting guest. A man, big and broad and Danish, who spoke to me with the familiarity so characteristic for people whose entire population is less than a fourth of the city of Mumbai. We got onto the small aeroplane that is to fly us the three hours it will take to bring us to the area in western Tanzania. One part of me is glad that I am on this aeroplane, for I am on my way back to things I love so much. Still, I worry about the time I will be away from you and what time will feel like without you. If you will remember me when I come back. I am not worried that you will not be loved while I am away. My mother has flown out from Scandinavia, knowing that this would give me freedom to return to the bush for a few days. Your father is there too, and Laito and Bahati. Not to mention Amadi, who takes you on your bird watch every morning at seven. You sit on top of his shuka clad arm and I see you sailing away through the gap in the curtain, every morning. The two of you always walk straight towards the sun, where it rises over the side of the mountain, and it looks as if you will both be swallowed by the horizon. Half an hour later I hear your crisp sounds and his too and you are delivered back to me to have a 1000 kisses and breakfast.

I will miss the feeling of you in the morning, when I lay your sleepy body on my chest and your arms and legs just flop down on each side, like a thick, hot chapati.

When I was pregnant people told me I would be more afraid for my life after having you. That I would rethink hunting buffalos. I don't think like this, for I don't go to the bush because of danger. I go there to breathe. Instead, I just wish I could have you with me in the bush. I wish everything was not made up of rules by men. Why could you not be in camp in the day while I was out hunting, surrounded by loving Tanzanians? Bahati could have been on the plane, too. There is plenty of space. Why not really? To keep up illusions, I guess. A baby's cry back in camp, when they would like to have a whiskey by the camp-fire, would destroy their ideas of having an alpha male experienced in the bush.

While you were having a nap the other day, your grandmother said to me;

"It is all thoughts, really, isn't it? Life is just a bunch of thoughts, nothing else."

She is right, of course, and so many of them are about making reality fit with an image someone wants of themselves, or the life they are leading, instead of trying to get closer to the core of some sort of truth. They say we are born naked and that we die naked, but I do not see it like that. We are born into circumstances that dress you from top to toe, and unless you spend your life undressing layer by layer, you will probably never experience the freedom of dying naked.

OCTOBER

Rungwa Inyonga hunting block, Western Tanzania

Every time I come back to the bush, I wonder why I left. I don't understand the disloyalty of my mind. The fickleness. The quick shift of heart. Here I laugh louder, here I sleep deeper. I wish you were with me, that is all. I miss you terribly.

When we have shot a buffalo, we spend the next hour teasing each other while taking off the skin, cutting up the meat and recounting old stories. Out here it hits me again that I have not written down enough of the things I have seen in the bush over the years, so far. When go back to the other world, I forget most of it, until I am back in the bush again.

Why, for instance, have I not taken notes in my diary about old Iddi and the stories he told me about being a Sandawe child? The intricate cruelties the Sandawe would do to the government officials, sent out to stop them from being the hunter-gatherers they had been for longer than anybody else on this earth. He described how, as children, they would go over to the hut where the pestering government official was sleeping. Slowly, they would excavate a small hole with a stick in the hut wall, pretending to play innocently. Then go back home and tell the one carrying a small poison arrow and wait for nightfall. There would be no cries in the night, no one shouting blue murder, no one discussing it, or even speaking of it. The government official just would not wake up again. The hyenas would see to the rest and they themselves could just continue living their calm lives.

Iddi was already in his early seventies when I met him in the bush. Standing no taller than my shoulder, as is typical of the true hunter-gatherer tribes, he still walked as fast and for as many hours as I. He could neither hear nor see very well anymore, but he was good company and saw nature in the same way as I. He worked with the company as a tracker and this was his last year, he told me.

Once, while brushing my hair outside my tent, I decided to have him on. It was the hair I pulled out of my brush, a dusty, matte blonde that had more or less the exact colour of a lion's mane that gave me the idea. It was a scorching afternoon and everybody was resting for an hour after lunch. I cut the tangled hair mane-size of an old lion and hung it on a few different bushes around my tent. It had rained a bit earlier, so I did not care that there were no visible tracks, then I called Iddi.

As he neared my tent, followed by a younger tracker, I put on a very excited expression on my face and said: "Iddi, look, a massive old lion has been here." He walked over to the place I was pointing at and lifted the hair from the bush. He slowly stretched it out to its full length: "Yes," he said and automatically looked towards the ground, to see if there were any tracks. "It rained earlier. It must have been here in the night," I said. He said nothing, but kept looking at the hair for a few moments longer while rubbing it between his fingers. Then his eyes started shifting from the hair to my head and back a few times. "It's too soft," he said disappointedly and put it in my hand. He didn't laugh, like I had expected him to. Instead, he looked up at me and said: "You have called the lion now." I laughed. "Iddi, the lions are all around us. I don't need to call one." He said: "You will see."

The next day, I walked straight into two sleeping lions. They were under a bush and I only noticed them when I was a few metres away. Iddi was not far behind me and I silently signalled for him to move backwards slowly. Had the lions woken up in that moment, when we were that close, they could have possibly charged and I would have had to shoot, or worse, things would have happened. It was incredible that they did not wake up. It must have been because the wind was strong in our faces. We slowly walked backwards until we were far enough. When I finally turned, Iddi looked at me with an expression in his eyes that was a mixture of anger and righteousness. "I told you, mama," he said.

If it was not for you, and a very few other people, I would not mind staying out here for an indefinite amount of time. It is the metamorphosis that is painful. The Natasha who lives in a tent with you and your father on a farm, the writer and mother and lover, does not quite seem to understand the Natasha out here, vice versa.

I dreaded coming out here this time. I feared this world of buffalos and madeyed poachers. Now that I am here, I am fearing going back to my life as a writer.

In the bush are those of my friends who will naturally and happily walk into any adventure and danger with me, albeit we do not necessarily know much of each other's private lives. Once we step into the track of a buffalo, everything between us rests on an unspoken absolute belief that we can follow the same rhythm and instinct in the unfolding of a hunt.

Chat-less bonds of trust to the death, tied together by hours and days and months of one foot in front of the other. A hunter's day is silent in words until a fem moments before resting midday and when back in camp in the evenings. But we still communicate the whole day, with our eyes, hands, and low whistles. These are people I would go into a war with. I know we would stick together in a battle.

Whenever I think a new person could become a close friend, I imagine us hunting a wounded buffalo or being in a war together. Once this film plays inside my head, I immediately see who would be who out there. Most people run away.

OCTOBER

My child, unspeakable things have happened out here in the bush since I was here last.

Unspeakable.

It seems like a systematic eradication of a species.

At first I just noticed a few small things that just looked like normal stark realities of nature. One small elephant calf walking about on its own, clearly confused and lost, another dead, lions at its side feasting on it. But then there was another again, having died in a mud hole, inches away from water, and another in the next waterhole, also being eaten by lions. Elephant cows are fierce, calves are no easy prey, not that easy. Then there were tracks of a single small elephant crossing the buffalo tracks we were following, then crossing again later on. Tracks of a lost calf walking in circles.

The horror slowly appeared, the stinking, rotten vision of mass slaughter by the most ruthless kind of poachers.

We had just successfully hunted one old buffalo bull, and I had noticed a curious thing on the watch I always had hanging from my hunting belt. The time on it had changed from our normal time to Swahili time. In Swahili time, the clock follows the hours of the days and of the night. Thus, when you would look at your watch and see that it says 7. Am, we would call it 1 o'clock, as 7 is the first entire hour of sunlight. 7 pm it is the first hour of darkness, so we call it 1 o'clock again.

Perfectly logical, when you live on the equator.

We spoke about it the mysterious time change of my watch while having our lunch in the scant shade of a tree. We went through all possibilities of how this could have happened, but nothing made sense. It was always connected to my belt and no one could have touched it. I was teased for being superstitious, but not too insistently. The people know me here; they see my habits and rules in the bush. Still they remember what their fathers believed about nature before the missionaries made them believe in the ultimate white guy. They know I believe what their fathers believed. The hunting-guest, who today is one of my close friends, was more sceptical at first. But eventually, having gone over the details again and again, even he had to admit that I was either lying, or this simply did not have a logical explanation.

The next day we followed buffalos again, but did not get even close to one. The day after that, we followed new tracks and did not get close to one either. This continued for days and days. It was always old bachelor bulls we followed. The tracking always started off well, but then the wind would change, or it would get hot unusually early and they would go into deep thickets, or we would be upon them in thick bush and they would rush out just in front of us, or onto the other side and disappear before we could react.

Every time the hunt would stop in the same way; with us next to carcasses of poached elephants. At first tracking the buffalo took us to one old, dead elephant, then two.

Eventually, many unsuccessful days later, our hunt finally led us to an entire herd of dead elephants. They lay scattered not very far from each other, their bodies all turned in the same direction as fallen dominos. Their grey skin blotched in vulture shit and their bodies concave.

A despair strong enough to weaken my knees washed over me and I put down my gun. I sat down by an elephant cow, in the middle of the slaughtered herd, and wept like a child while staring into the ground. Beside her was the dead calf who had stayed, who had dried and slowly shrunk into death, whilst all about it had already died a day or two before. Its face was intact because it had no ivory yet. It had died of thirst and hunger next to its mother. My mind waded through elephant carcasses and could not find a way out. The guest didn't cry, but sat still and stared into the void with an apocalyptic expression on his face. At one stage, we looked into each other's eyes for a long time, saying nothing. We both knew that this had changed something in us both. He didn't say a word, but I saw his inner dialogue flit across his face like on a film canvas. Shifting expressions that finally landed resolutely and formed a gigantic promise.

Someone, I don't know who, touched my shoulder to motion for us to leave. I wanted to bite his hand. I looked around the herd and knew how it had been. One shot to the knee and you have the elephant immobilised. When I saw the biggest bull among them, I mourned not only for it, but for the mortality of my father too. For each of the dead calves, I also mourned for you. Spread out all over the dust clearing they had made from running in wild chaos and terror, I imagined each of them going down.

Like babushkas of all sizes and ages, opened in the middle and fallen out of each other, and quite forgotten in a place where no one might ever have walked by.

One day, there were shots nearby. A blind anger in me made me walk towards the sound while imagining a shot directed towards me, so I could fire back, but images of you without me and one tracker held me back. Day after day, the buffalo brought us up to dead elephants then vanished. I felt both drawn and scared to meet the poachers.

It was as if we were wading around in a repetitive dream. Again and again the same. The buffalo that we tracked for hours and hours that then vanished, and left us near dead elephants. I knew that Mungu porini, the spirit of nature, was telling me something, was asking me to see. The trackers were not laughing anymore when I said it to them. We all saw what we saw. Every day. For days and days. We fell completely silent. It was shameful to be a human being, and we stopped looking at each other.

One day I changed the clock back from Swahili time and told everyone that I did it. The nightmare stopped immediately. We heard no more shots. The buffalo stopped taking us to dead elephants. Next day we hunted a buffalo with ease. The message had been received. Nothing, however, went back to how it was before. Your face and babu's face and the dead elephants intermingled in my tossing and turning nights. I never could sleep properly around the time of the full moon. Now, between nightmares, I sat outside my tent and cried and spat onto the ground with frustration. I hated and mourned. I never hated before.

I have not forgotten this slaughter.

I will do what I can for the elephants now, I promise you that, my love. How otherwise could I tell you I am a hunter and still look you in the eyes? How otherwise could I stop imagining my father being ashamed of me and my grandfather turning in his grave? Real hunters believe in balance. In never taking too much and giving more back than what they have taken.

I will not let us down.

OCTOBER

Losemingore Mountains, northern Tanzania
I am in my most favourite area, hunting the mountain buffalo of Losemingore.

I have left you, but only for ten days this time, and I am only a drive away.

Three weeks was too long. I will not go away from you for that long for some years again, my love. It felt unnatural and I have a bad conscience about it. But I had to try it to know. I know now that 21 day safaris are out for the time being. 10 days is the limit. You were happy and fat in my arms again after those three weeks, but when I looked into that open, trusting face, I knew to not go away for that long again for some years.

Out here I fall a sleep well and wake up strong. It is not a bigger feeling than waking up in the middle of the night at home, to a storm outside, and seeing you, my new eternal love, by my side. It is, however, a magical one. I am out here fetching health for myself, a salary and food, all of which I bring home to us. It gives me a quite natural feeling of belonging and accomplishment. One humans have had for thousands of years.

I leave to return with quarry for us both and a calm sense of roots.

I swiftly walk out of camp at first light or wait patiently behind the sweeping hem of the lifting mist. The time we walk out all depends on the whims of the day.

On these mountains, thankfully, there are no elephant poachers.

We hunt every day, but if one old bull buffalo is shot in ten days, it has been a very successful safari. Sometimes, we come down from the mountain empty handed, but with clear eyes and broad smiles.

When the sun is too hot or the sun is in zenith so the shadow in the tracks disappears, we stop under the most generous tree. we rest, drink and eat something. Then we take a tsetse fly-swatting, sweat-bee waving midday slumber. Sleep arrives when a rare gust of wind passes under the trees. Once you have fallen asleep, tiredness keeps you, until you wake up wet with sweat forty-five minutes later. The animals and I and the man I am hunting with, for the hunting guest, are nearly always men, sleep when the animals sleep and hunt when the animals are awake. When all life ebb into islands of shade, for a few hours, millions of acres of Tanzanian bush lay resting and free from hooves and feet and grazing lips. Then, just before the day cools, we stand up and continue the hunt again until nightfall.

It can be hours, or days, or a week, but more often than not, an old buffalo bull falls. Most often, it was the bullet of someone else that killed it. But I am the one who tracked it, carefully pointed it out for being an old male and therefore suitable quarry, and that is how it came to death. Only if it is wounded and is about to get away, or if it is charging, or is about to charge, do I shoot. So far, I have been the one to appear again on the other side of that grass. Depending on the level of experience of the hunting guest, he either goes with me and the tracker into the thicket, or not. It is not only because I want the guest to be safe. It is just as much that I could not bear it should he get harmed, to carry the regret of that for the rest of my life.

After the shot, I wait twenty minutes before going up to the animal.

Hopefully now, the death bellow of the buffalo.

Then the parting of the meat. There is the gathering of flies and butterflies and bees that all so love the blood. Sometimes a bit later, there is the smell of the smoke and the fire and the liver on a stick sliced off, bit by bit, until the last piece falls off on its own. I reach for the heart in the animal's chest and cut the tip off and walk away with it. I hold it for a moment. Think about how it was beating a few moments ago and recognise my responsibility in stopping it. I thank mungu porini and repeat my promise to always try to give more back to nature that what I take for the rest of my life. I repeat, I will be its eyes and ears, if only it will speak to me and show me what I must know and do. I throw the tip of the heart back into the forest, or over the bush landscape, with all of my strength. Back to that which I believe is into the force that set it pumping.

Then I lie down and rest for a while on the ground under a shady tree. Eventually, all of its body, inside and out, is carried on our backs and heads, uphill, downhill, back to camp. For a few hours, we stop whispering and talk in normal voices. We celebrate with laughter and recount the days and the things we went through to get our quarry.

My days up here are spent smelling, seeing and hearing, making myself small, silent and slow, while searching for the senses that we do not have proper names for. Mostly, it is about just being quiet, not saying anything at all.

There is no past, neither is there a future, when you hunt like this.

The unfolding of thin layers of the present through your senses.

At nightfall, to the sound of scops owls and bush babies, your mother writes a bit in her tent, then falls asleep and sleeps well.

If you dislike my story, I am truly sorry. In the life of your mother, it is like this.

Death in all manners and forms, our own and that of other animals, doesn't have very many good arguments on its side any more. It's terribly unpopular, I know. Urbanised man, unaffected by the reality of life, has begun building a massive case against it, in the ambitious hope of one day putting it away for good.

We are entering the age of the great disconnect to the land, my darling. This is just the beginning of this era. Some people have hate for hunters like me, but that is only because no one has proven yet that vegetables are also connected enough to life to sense when it is taken from them. That will be awhile yet, so they will keep shouting louder and louder about people like me.

The mooring lines that tie us to the realities of nature are being gnawed at, the sails are being hoisted to take us into the endless sea of cyberspace.

An entire language will be lost when the last hunter is finally poached out by an urbanised man. When one day they realise that no animal can live without taking life, be it animal or vegetable matter, it will be too late to rekindle that language. Urbanised man will by then have taken us away, lifted us from the soil for good and taken us out of the food chain. When you no longer understand the language of nature, because you just regard it, and no longer live off and in it, true communication with it stops. Putting it on a pedestal, or raping and pillaging it becomes the norm instead.

There was a moment the other day, when the flesh of a buffalo was all parted and the guts rolled out by my feet to be cleaned, that I realised we are all beginning to put ourselves in an impossible situation, for even my heart now sometimes shies away from what I know to be natural. Even I now have moments of shame for being an animal.

It might be during your lifetime that the notion of people having killed animals and eaten them will be perceived as an absurd and cruel part of history. My conservation arguments will not matter at all. It will not matter if I say that hunting in the year of now was very much necessary for the survival of the wilds of Tanzania, or that hunters keep wilderness where vegetarians keep wheat fields. It will not matter because too much of this reality will be forgotten in the history books, and what is left is a story told in the context and with the emotion of that present time. What was lost at this moral shift will also not be mentioned or even fathomed. People will not know anymore.

Something is always lost in the moral shifts of history. Sometimes, part of what was lost was crucial, beautiful, or had a certain knowledge about something that could have helped protect us later. Only then does the question "how did we end up here" arise. It is a little like taking medicine. It is fantastic that medicine exists, and often it saves lives. But we rarely talk about the good things that are killed in our body each time we take medicines to stop disease.

We don't live for long enough to grow empathy towards our own history. The mystery of the past, the fallacy of historical judgement, will always be that the present cannot access the reality of what it was like then. Human history is judged on false premises of circumstance by default.

When hunting has been closed, the next step from there is to not kill animals for consumption at all. From there, we might eventually agree to not kill vegetables. At least then it all makes more sense to me. Then, for a moment, we might see that all life is life. We will most probably one day stop cutting flowers, and trees to build houses, forbid keeping animals in cages, pens or stables, after that to not draw anything from them, neither their milk, nor their eggs, nor their wool or honey. Then we must stop riding horses and using donkeys, for we can't pretend that this is anything else than animal exploitation and animal slavery, if we are honest.

This dream of a pain-free and deathless world, will it convince us we can be the gods we so want to be? For that is the ultimate game. That we can convince ourselves that we are worthier than the other animals, that we are higher than them and don't kill.

But what will happen when science discovers that everything that a human has ever eaten, with an exception of salt, has lived? Will we then sacrifice our species and let ourselves die of starvation? Or accept death again?

I am a hunter. Nowhere do I feel more natural than in the tracks of a buffalo. I am sorry, my darling, but that is how it is. It is awful to see an animal die. No hunter will tell you anything else. Hunters rarely speak of it, but they do feel it. To see the light taken out of the eyes of a living creature is nothing but terrible. It is the reality of being a meat eater, a leather wearer, a child bearer in an overflow of humans, even existing at all.

It is the blunt truth that we cannot exist without killing. Killing cannot be avoided. The question is what and how much and what you give back and what you protect and how many children you have. A true hunter believes in balance, nothing more and nothing less. Don't mix up the hunter with the killer. They are mortal enemies.

You will rarely see me kill a fly, in the literal sense. And as natural as it is for me to hunt, as natural is it to give all I can to protect wildlife and natural tracts of land.

We mock and despise past generations for their moral and ethical decisions, yet forget that premises, beliefs and values are still shifting.. Nothing is constant. Nothing stops changing. Evolution that will stretch over the entire future of life is not a promise of betterment, but a promise of change. What are you doing now that your children will despise? Some behaviour or morals seem acceptable to us for five generations, some last much less or more, but they keep changing.

I am sorry that you land in a minute of time, where you might hate how your mother spent her life. What about the silences and lifted eyebrows you will have to deal with when you tell others that your mother was a hunter in Africa?

Maybe it will change when modern man understands that a natural life and balance is the hunter's aim, and that all that lives kills Directly or indirectly. Unless we lie. I might be awfully popular in your grandchildren's time in history. Who knows?

NOVEMBER

Oldonyo sambu, Tanzania

I am back home. You are in my arms again. I am in want of nothing and cannot fathom how I ever could. There is a storm shaking our home and at one point we go outside in case the roof will come flying off. Later that day, there is a slight earth tremour and President Nyerere falls to the floor and breaks his frame.

NOVEMBER

Southern Spain

We went to Spain to take your babu from the hospital. To bring him to his home after the operation.

He is rude to most of the nurses, and absolutely adores one of them. The one he adores says he has beautifully shaped, long legs.

You learnt to walk, right there, just next to where he was lying in his hospital bed, refusing to take another bite of food. You took your first steps on the floor, where your babu took his last.

Imagine what those feet of your babus have touched. They have walked all over the earth, have been to places where some of them do not even exist anymore. We are twice as many now, since he was living in the African, South American, and Asian forests.

Last summer by the coast in Sweden, we had lunch with your father's family. "There is nothing like shooting eight or ten Macaw parrots on an evening in the jungle," he said, and looked down at his plate for a moment, like he did when he had said something unusual. Some people modify how things were, when things are not like that anymore, but not your babu.

"It was when I lived in the forest in Brazil in the late fifties and the Indians came to me and begged me to get some feathers for their ceremonial dress-code." Then he would secretly look at their faces and humour himself about their disgusted expressions. I think he found much greater pleasure in that, than talking about the pieces of land and the many species of animals he and his father had saved from extinction. He kept that to himself.

As he slowly got up from his hospital bed and walked to the bathroom, you grabbed hold of his bathrobe to pull yourself up. He stopped for a moment. Your little hand held on, pulled the one side of his robe down a little and you threw me a glance and smile, proud of your efforts. He put a hand on your head and looked down at you, as if to say: "Yes, this is how it is supposed to go. It is right, like this."

Then the two of you walked off in opposite directions to explore something entirely unknown to each. One just arrived and one almost leaving. There wasn't much you could have taught each other about the other side of the front door right now, anyway. Your memory was still too fresh from the place that you came from, a place he could not remember. His mind was full of the place he had been in for the last 77 years, a place you hardly understood yet.

The doctors told me he was fine. He, however, told me he was not.

Already the year before, when you were three weeks old, he started preparing me. He came out to see you here in Tanzania and we all went to the coast. Here he sat on a veranda looking at birds most of the day. Few birds had passed in his life that he had not noticed, never was he alone. There was always a speck in the sky, a sound from a tree, that told him and later told us that someone we recognised or someone we did not know yet, was there. He used to laugh at people who would just walk through a forest and "not see a bloody thing." People who have neither accepted hunting, nor planted or saved the life of anything here.

He told me that this was the last time he was in Africa. With a knot in my stomach, I asked him why. He gave me a menacing look, one I'd seen before. It was clear he would not let me contradict. He was irritated when he saw tears forming in my eyes. But then he remembered I was his child, and he softened his voice just in time before the words came out:

"Natasha, when you have lived as much as I have.. When you have seen and experienced as much as I have, lived in the places during the spectacular times that I have, a day comes when you are full. I refuse to be an old fool." We have spoken about it many times before. "You are a hunter and must understand this. You cannot let me become a doddering, old fool. Do you remember the conversation we had about what to do with the other if we were in a coma? I wanted three months, and you wanted six before the machine should be turned off. Time is near. I had enough. Accept it, Natasha, and don't argue so much. Besides, I can't do those long aeroplane flights anymore."

I closed my heart around the last sentence. There was hope in those words. He laughed and raised his voice and said,

"Now go and get your Daddy a cup of tea, then come back and loose to me in backgammon, and tell me who that bird is."

"A palm-nut vulture," I said and looked at it as it flew past us, following the coastline.

"You see? Even *I* am still learning. Considering how damned clever I am, that's not such a straightforward task," he said and laughed.

I felt connected to him there. In my fear of losing him, I was glad that we had spent so many hours over the last forty years casting our gaze out to wings passing by when we were together. Those flying creatures had drawn silken lines that created a web, now all around and above us and spun together in an inextricable pattern that not even death could extract us from.

"But are you sick?"

"No, not really," he said. "That is not what I am talking about."

NOVEMBER

You will experience it; the helplessness you feel when a parent packs his or her bags to go somewhere for work or a social event.

You try to tell them they must not go, that they must not leave you behind, even if is only for a day. You cry and shout and refuse any kind of bribe, but still they go. They have to, they tell you. Slowly, as it sinks in, the power shuts down and the moon loses its gravitational hold over earth. They don't seem to notice.

The world rolls away, like a ball through the universe, past aphelion, light dimming. There is nothing you can do while they slowly fold their shirts and lay them down, one on top of the other, first on the bed. Then from there they press stacks of them, as if to fit one more shirt, one more day away from you, down in to their big, dark suitcases. It takes a bit of time when they put their shoes in soft bags. Each shoe is both a delicious and an anxious delay. Then they close the bags gently by pulling a string. You wonder why the shoes would have to be so polished. How come the shoes can come and you cannot? When did they polish them, anyway? A long time ago? You did not see it done. Maybe at night when you were sleeping, is when they did it, you think. It is all a premeditated crime you realise then, intricately planned long before you were told about any of it.

They fill up the car with things and chatter and drive off, just leaving behind puffs of scent and notes on the pillow. The beam from the headlights, the sound fades and the car itself shrinks in front of your eyes as they speed off and leave you to deal with dusk and silence. They stop one more time down the road, when they are about half-size and half-sound. Then they open the windows on both sides and stick their arms out and wave to you. Once more you hear their horn honking, weakly now. They drive on again and this is when you remember that there was something you forgot to tell them. You form the words silently and stand there for a moment longer, in case they should have forgotten something and need to come back and pick it up. Or in case they will wave again, one very last time, before they disappear all-together.

NOVEMBER

Yesterday we took your babu home from the small hospital in Spain. Today, we sat at his dinner table after I had put you to bed.

We played backgammon. I cried and told him it was because I was relieved that he was back home. Everything is going to be fine, I said. He picked up the dice and shook his head slowly from one side to the other. He did not throw them. Just held them in his hand. I love that hand. It was a gentle and steady hand, with one fingertip crushed between two timbers in Burma. A hand that has caressed mine often.

Sitting there in an old blue bathrobe, he gave me a scrutinising look. His face was deeply sunken. I have loved him so very much in my life so far; I have needed him when he was not there; I have feared him. He has hurt me so with his harsh, selfish behaviour. He has treated me cruelly at times and shouted the life out of me. He has loved me much and truly believed in me, too. Then he has explained to me that the biggest challenge of the wise, is to make your passions your work, or you waste your life like a fool. He has pressed one of my universal keys into my hand with a firm grip. Pressed it there until I knew how to hold on to it myself. The love for nature, the love for adventure. Then he has let me fly freely, without a question in the world. Early.

"Thank you, daddy," I say. "Thank you for the key that you gave me. It is the biggest gift I have had in my life from home, the love for nature and hunting. I guess because grandmother was who she was, there was nothing strange about my choices to you. I thought about that lately. Our history is my luck. Her time in India, the Himalayas, riding her motorbike to Paris, donning an English officer's uniform hair chopped off and all that. Thank God that you never had a son, too. Ha!

I thanked him for never having told me that others might think it strange that a girl wanted all the things I did. Like living in Tanzania in the middle of nowhere in a tent. That he never questioned it. That he never showed me any fear for me.

"Had you been killed by a buffalo, I would have known that you died free and happy and doing what you wanted, simple as that," he said, looking up at me, firmly. Then he added, a bit later: "But don't you dare. I go first. Parents go first, then the children."

I told him I only discovered when I was halfway to becoming a professional hunter that others differed from us. That they divided life choices into male and female categories. I thanked him for speaking to me about animals, hunting and life, instead of asking me about my safety or ever doubting my dreams to have a life in the bush in Tanzania. I told him that this was what made me feel safe in the first place, that he didn't ask me, but just accepted and let me live. "Most fathers don't do that. It was the biggest support I could ever have asked for in my life."

"I don't think I discouraged you, nor did I encourage you, did I? I think it was more that I did not care enough at the onset of it all. I wasn't concentrating on you."

I could not tell if there was regret in those words or if they were just matter-of-factly. My throat tightened. His brown eyes were big. He looked at me with a stare. I wanted to run away at those harsh words. I had misunderstood something massive. At the same time, I got that feeling now, of a parent packing, and I didn't want to hear him say another word. But he said nothing. We just looked at each other like that for a moment. Both stubbornly not wanting to look down first.

We spent 41 and a half years looking at all the animals of the ark together. There are so many different kinds of birds, fish, insects that a lifetime is not enough to discuss all of them. Together we looked them up in books. We have met quite a few of them together. We eagerly discussed which ones can do what, where they live, where they come from, how to hunt them, or how to not hunt them and protect them from man.

Now, when we spoke of them, he answered my questions half heartedly and argued with lukewarm interest, as if he was preparing to put them away for good. I imagined him picking them up one by one now, as if he wanted to put them into a bag and carry them all back to the ark.

I told him to stop dying. He didn't mildly tell me off. He roared at me that I had to accept that he would not eat another thing. I roared back. We had a war about his living or not. I was for and he was against. There was nothing kind about my words, his neither. He was going to leave, he told me. He slapped the table with his hand, with the words that he had little to live for anymore. I ignored the steel cold stabs of his words. Forcefully, I tried to stop him from packing his lifetime up, but he pushed me away and angrily told me he had no more room in his life. That he had already filled every single little space in it.

And so I sat down again and shut up. I watched him. What else could I do?

I stubbornly pulled a few of the animals back out again and put them in front of us. I told him I just saw this one in real life, asked him how it was to rear that one. He couldn't stand European herring gulls, he told me. He had dreamt a lot about them lately. They wanted to pull him down into the darkness. "Damn herring gulls, I always hated them." He said, and we both laughed insecurely and looked at each other for a long time.

I told him a story from my last buffalo hunt. I told it with as many details as I could find. Told him how the ground felt under my feet that day. What we had in our lunchbox. What species of birds we had seen. I spent half an hour describing the last fifteen minutes before the two buffalo came charging out of the shrub and directly towards us. I told him about the elephants too for hours and hours, without stopping.

He listened calmly now. Sat quite still. But I could see that he was shaking his head at me somehow. His beautiful mouth was serious, his eyes soft. He suspected I was trying to manipulate him into forgetting the hour, like children do, when it is already far too late. He tried to communicate to me that the moment had come for me to accept what time it was. That it was bedtime. That no more time could be bargained for. No more stories would be told. That it was "lights out". Then he spoke to me and looked at me as if he knew what time it was and that I didn't. And it is true, I didn't want to know. I just knew that I din't want him to leave. He told me he could have never hunted an elephant. I cried about the elephants. I told him I thought they might be gone for good soon and he silently nodded with that faraway expression in his brown eyes that always reminded me of a sad child. He told me he loved me.

And so he seemed to sigh and laugh a little. As if to say: "OK, one more round then," and I trusted him and went back to Africa, knowing that I would see him soon again.

The seconds of a life have led to minutes, to years, to decades.

With a hiss, the biggest wheel in the calendar clock turns over that one single time of a lifetime, and finally falls in to place with a cold "clonk," to mark the end of a life.

There are no mistakes in such a finely tuned machine. Never any stumbling here.

YEAR TWO

JANUARY

Skåne, Southern Sweden.
We are in Sweden to bury your babu. We have all left the hill, the almost unbearable heat of Tanzania, and have taken up residence for Christmas and new year in a small castle belonging to one of my oldest childhood friends in Sweden. Ironically, he and his wife have gone to Tanzania on a trip that involved seeing us. I am working on a poem to read at his funeral. I feel sick about those of his friends who will not make it to the lakeside in Småland, where he will be buried next to his father. We always spoke openly about death, so there are no doubts about what he wanted us to do with his body.

Charging buffalos, intent on killing me, have taught me nothing about death, instead have they have showed life.

Previous devastating losses to death have taught me nothing, either.

Your father is here, next to me, but I cannot reach his heart, more than I could ever reach the stars. My fear and pain and loneliness make me react to the smallest things. Anything he does, that I did not know he would do, fills me with worry of what ominous things it might mean. I have lost my normal emotional maps. I can't quite keep things apart. It is not only the death of my father. I have been alone, have felt abandoned by your father for too long now. I no longer know the difference between what is my hunger for his care and nearness, and being full to the brim with sorrow and abandonment. I am full and hungry at the same time. A terrible feeling that takes me to an emotional delirium, surely much like the fata morgana a man crawling through the desert. To never know when to trust what you think you see or not, but to still just keep stumbling forward.

For the first time, I know what it is like, the thing I have only touched upon with fear for the last fifteen years of my life - to lose a parent. It will not be a pretty thing for you either, my girl. The image of you crying by my grave might even keep me alive longer, now that I know what it feels like. But there is also some kind of natural consolation in death being in the right order.

Your babu died in this the same year that I saw the elephants falling.

The last months I have stood on a shuddering ground while giants keep crashing down around me and the ground is whirled up and away with the dust devils.

We go outside often, you and I, facing the mercilessly flat and windy farm fields of southern Sweden. I took a walk with you today, tucked into a sheepskin sleeping bag in your stroller, and you fell asleep within minutes. The time before last that I spoke to your babu on the telephone, I told him I had shot my first fox with a rifle. I still remember how that fox looked at me as it trotted past. I should not have shot it. There was a certain secret moment between us, but my hunting instinct was faster than my heart.

I keep thinking his death somehow has to do with the death of that fox and the death of the elephants. I should not have shot that fox. I only should hunt buffalo. We pass over a little bridge at the edge of some fields. The water is still open underneath us, between the icy edges. I wonder if it is just below freezing or colder.

He died when he felt the time had come. His last act was life affirming. He politely gave his place here back when it seemed appropriate to him, seemingly without fear of what was to come. I wish I hadn't argued with him about it. I should have supported his very solid decision to leave, as opposed to trying to make him stay. One of my best friends that I spoke to on the telephone yesterday said: "It is typical of your stubborn lot. You will do the same thing."

I thought a lot about how your babu's forehead felt when I kissed it after I arrived in Spain. I was eleven and a half hours late to say goodbye to him, you see.

When our kitchen, there in the middle of our desert, filled with the most incredible smell of flowers, I knew. I got on the plane in Kilimanjaro while he was alive. Still, I was too late.

I always loved the place where his forehead met his white hair. Stroking that place was the last thing I did when I said goodbye to his body for the last time. I would have never dared to do that when he was alive. I respected his hierarchical place too much to do such a motherly thing to my father. There was a certain boy-like character to the way the hair turned from his forehead right there. A certain innocence to that bend of hair, so in contrast to his loud bass voice. His hair never fell out, but stayed with him all his life, changing slowly from raven black to white. Like the land under my feet in the course of one Swedish cycle of seasons. Black, heavy, living mould in spring, white, everything hidden away in the snow now. He used to say that it was a lucky thing that he was not the type to go bald. Heads like his were not supposed to be naked, his ears being too big and the shape of his skull all too long and narrow, he had decided. So it was how it was meant, he told us. "Those who lose their hair do so, because they can afford to."

Kissing his forehead when I saw him the last time was like kissing a marble wall, a cold, strong, impenetrable divide that let no sound, no smell, no light through. I stood on my side and that wall that rose solidly between my lips and him and refused to let even the smallest of messages through to my father. "I got your last message though," I told his still face." I heard you. It is OK. I understand."

On the flight from Kilimanjaro, one sentence kept coming to me. It came to me louder and louder. Finally, I had to go to the back of the plane and write it down. I knew I was writing about the coming death of my father. I had instinctively known for several hours by then.

"Don't you see," came the impatient words, "don't you see that I have to go? The migratory birds have left. I am already late. I am already late."

We were both late. He for death and I for his last bit of life.

The fastest way for me to get to Malaga from Kilimanjaro was strangely through Kastrup. When I came to the house of your father's family in Southern Sweden that night, waiting for the morning flight on to Spain, your babu died.

But the migratory birds made it after all, before the worst of winter that year, and when I opened my bag the next morning, the first thing I saw was a feather on top of my clothes.

When I spoke to your aunt about that later, she told me that one of the last things she had spoken to our babu about was the picture above his bed. A painting we had known all our lives. He was already very weak then. It had been painted by an old Swedish nature painter and it portrayed two swans flying over open water. "What are the birds doing?" he had asked her. "They are just flying in circles there," she answered fearfully. "No," he said, "they are not. Can't you see? They are migrating. They are going away now."

I found a jasmine under your aunt's chair on the hospital veranda minutes after I had said goodbye to your babu. I heard them open the doors to his room to roll him out to go to the flames. Of course, it was the smell of jasmine I had had in the kitchen at home in Oldonyo Sambu, I thought, and picked it up.

"Your father loved jasmines," my mother said. I got up and walked around the garden. There were no jasmine bushes there, though, no other visitors in the tiny private hospital that it was.

To hell with people who think I am over-interpreting things, and those who think badly of the things they do not understand. To not give a damn is something I will have to teach you already in kindergarten. I am not sure how the opportunity will show itself, but it won't be long because people are very generous with their opinions, as soon something is one millimetre off the beaten track. Most of their views should not concern you in the slightest.

"The day you learn how to trust your instincts, against all logic, and follow them with conviction, is the day you become a good hunter." That was what he said, the old hunter. I was still a young apprentice in Tanzania. Had only ever had one client. Now I was just tagging along with the old master, hoping to catch some last minute tips. Soon there would only be solo flying left for me.

"You wait here, with the client. I will be back in a moment. I just have to…" His whisper trailed off. He had already turned around and was walking backwards, on the same tracks we had followed up to there. I looked down and clearly saw that we were still on the tracks and that they carried on in front of us. The buffalo that the guest had wounded had stayed with the herd and we were following it, had for hours already. I took a step out of the high grass, my thumb on the safety catch, and waited, not understanding why we did not just keep following the tracks forward.

A while later, two shots were heard nearby, in quick
succession. It was from his double rifle, "The old spout," as he
called it. We stood there in the midday sun for another half
an hour, when his slight body appeared in front of us again
and he told us he had shot the buffalo. That evening, when I
asked him what he had seen to go back, he told me, "I saw
nothing. No tracks or anything like that. I just knew it, like
you will, if you learn to follow your instincts."

Once you have learned the technique about anything, my
darling, unlearn it to a degree again, ignore some of the ideas
of "fact" that science has muffled truth with.

JANUARY

Then the other day, your father said: "Will you write about
me too, please?"

I had not planned to. Not for any other reason, other than
wanting to protect his integrity. Of course, most people
understand not to say such a thing to a writer.

Where should I begin? That we are alone again on top of
this hill, him having left? This time, possibly for good. Or
what my love for him looks like? Yes, this will be what you are
looking for; what my love for him looks like.

Imagine that my love for your father was an animal and it
would have looked like a bear, with massive wings and its
short tail that of a fish. An animal who looks very unlikely,
comical, clumsy possibly, oh, but ready to take on anything
with its strange body. My attempt to be in his life was a
struggle to command all these limbs at once.

My love for him then could have done almost anything,
but the problem was that he did not notice my love inside his
own storm.

I am not sure he ever saw my love. If no one is watching,
anything can undo itself to the absolute degree of never
having existed at all. You will kill something by not watching,
or you will create it by opening your eyes. The feeling of the
divine just comes from your ability to take in wholly. Don't
close your eyes, If you are hungry for life. Stare at the outline
in front of you until it starts breathing.

I know it is not a classically happy fairy tale I am telling
you here, but that does not mean it was not just all right and
how it was supposed to be.

What I got from your father is the greatest gift of all, and
what I gave him was the greatest gift of all. I could not have
had it from anyone else, and neither could he.

JANUARY.

My next book, I think I will start with the words: "The first
thing you have to do, when you understand how to do it, is to
ask yourself how you would like to die. When you know that,
you know how you want to live your life, too."

I admire a good bullfight in Las Ventas in the San Isidro of
Madrid, because I imagine I will have a passionate death
myself. I fear the slow wilting of the milked out cow. It is the
bull I admire. It is the tolerable death-moment of the bull that
I hope for. The good toreador is there to give the bull that, not
to conquer its life. No one gets away with living and neither
of us nor the bull gets to fight unto the death more than once.
It's not a sport or a competition, bullfighting. It is a simple

tragedy, both to live and watching a bullfight. The storyline and ending is always known, but is acted well or badly.

As far as competing concerned, I know that there is only one worth fighting to the death for. I know that the one who loves the most is the winner.

I think of my father's shirts. How they are perfectly ironed. How his socks are lined up in his drawers. His trousers still sheathed in the thin plastic from the dry cleaners hang neatly. It is all waiting to be used still. And then I think of how he died. Maybe it is the most natural thing imaginable for a man to decide that time has come. To simply walk over to the fire and give his spark back. He did just that. He decided that life had filled him sufficiently. So he stopped eating and died. Your great grandmother, his mother, did the same thing.

Maybe the hunter can be more understood after all, when they are impeccable hosts the day their own death comes and knocks on their front door.

FEBRUARY

We are staying your maternal grandmother's house for a few days before our return home to Tanzania. You are happy. You laugh and dance a lot while holding on to the furniture.

We are a jungle, your family on my side. Your father being more urbanised than us. Maybe you have a bigger chance of being like most people still. On my side we are a passionately concerned with animal life, animal death, dogs, horses, and every bird that passes over our heads and any insect that passes by. None of us would give the sound of a river up for a voice, and a forest is a place to talk to. We never speak of it, but I think we would all agree enthusiastically.

Your grandmother could be mistaken for being a bit more sober in that regard. She is fond of telling us all how she cannot fathom how one can get so attached to a dog as we all are. She mostly likes animals that remind her of humans. Like the orphaned chimpanzees and gorillas that she reared next to my sister when they lived in Cameroon. But any animal she has bottle fed are a different, mysterious exception to the rule. She truly is puzzled at how we are so fixated on rearing, saving, or hunting animals. But give her anything with roots, any seed with just a chance even to grow roots, and watch her kneel in front of it, with the thin excuse that she is kneeling to plant it. When we go and see her, we try to close doors and windows in her house and leaves and branches overwhelm themselves to come inside. If you reach for the garden scissors, you better have a damn good excuse. Being able to look out her windows will not be a good enough reason. She smuggles tomato seeds in her pockets and throws them around our home in Tanzania. Tomatoes are full of magic to her. In front of her door is a flower bed that you have to step over to enter her house. Her way of telling you to tread carefully and to understand that this is a home where plants live.

"You have no right to enjoy the arrival of a child, if you cannot accept death," she throws words like that next to me, like seeds to pigeons.

I don't know where she gets them from in February, but she just put a flower behind each of our ears. Maybe to tell us that things keep growing somewhere, even during this terribly cold winter.

FEBRUARY

Oldonyo sambu, Tanzania.

I am in a fog. My father just died. I told your father to move
out. All I can think of is how I keep all the pain that is seeping
from my pores, from you. I am on my knees grazing dust. At
least I know I can get back from there. It is something I have
done before. I have come back from even worse places.
Someone once said to me with anger and disappointment:
"You are such a goddamn survivor." I have to remember that
now, that I am a "goddamn survivor." This time I have you. It
can definitely be done just for that reason.

A scene keeps returning to my mind, that I am ashamed
of. I should not be, but I am still. I do not even remember
why it happened. You were not there, but with Laito at home.
We had only been away for half an hour. We had gone to get
kerosene for the hurricane lamps. The fight we had exhausted
me and made me drive slower and slower until the engine
stalled and the car just stood there, like a beetle having given
up climb the steep hill to our home. Then car doors were
open I walked outside. I was sitting on my knees behind it, in
the half metre velvet soft dust down from our hill, shouting
and begging something from your father. My legs were under
the powder dust completely and halfway up my hips. I am not
sure how I got there. He stood further away. The dust covered
my legs like a blanket and I felt like lying down and letting
myself be swallowed up by it entirely. A very tall Mwarusha
woman walked by on the other side of the small gully of
erosion, with firewood on her head. She stopped further away
and turned towards us. Then she stood there in her green

kanga, and I stared at her, knowing that she could not see my face properly. She put the firewood down. A dust devil slipped by and enveloped us all so I had to close my eyes and she shouted loudly through the dust and wind at him in Swahili; "Just forgive her. Please, just forgive her. Forgive her. Just forgive her."

I was not asking to be forgiven for anything. The distance between each of the three of us was over twenty metres. Then the dust devil covered all our lines of sight and for a moment. Three strangers stood in their own isolation with their own message, that neither of the others understood.

Thank God for Laito. He says little, and he understands everything about what is going on. He lifts you in his gentle hands and takes you for a walk, patiently talking to you about insects and plants and goats and cows. His voice is gentle like cool cotton. He brings a tray with tea at four and even when the entire world is rattling to pieces around us, he moves with steady calm.

I try to laugh and play with you, but you know. Hopefully, you will not remember later, but the look you sometimes give me is that of someone who is saying; "Don't do this. Don't lie to me. Why are you acting?"

I wanted to make things work with your father, but he opened shop with his demons. He is hardly ever here. He never really unpacked his bags, but landed and took off again in a great flap. Not much different from the shiny ravens who come to drink water outside our bedroom window, now and again. Beautiful, brilliant in some ways. But never to be regarded as anything else than a flighty creature in my life, that occasionally woke me up with its hard beaked tapping on the windows.

Your heart is yours, mine is mine. There are no sides to be chosen. Grow yourself fat from both your mother and your father. That is all you can and should do. Eat us, drink us up and grow.

FEBRUARY

There is a tree that when it has come to its full size, it cracks down the middle, exposing to the weather its innermost core. That is no problem when the weather is fair, but eventually it will rain a bit too long and the core will start softening and rotting. When that happens, a sort of signal is sent through the tree and one of the newest delicate shoots furthest out on one branch will turn up and bend inwards, until it finds the dying core, which is its own source of life. Slowly, this thin shoot of a branch will lower itself and plant itself into the mould of its forefather and take hold. Roots will start growing and as the old tree rots more and more, it becomes the most perfect compost for this the new tree to grow in.

In your babu's hospital room, you took your first victorious steps and he took his last. He passed you on the way to the bathroom, and you took hold of his dressing gown and pulled yourself up. He paused and put his hand on your head. There, in that moment, the old yew tree sent a message, and a little green shoot started its journey upwards and straight towards the core of its own dying tree.

MARCH

The generations still alive serve like rice doors between yourself and your own death. When my last grandparent died, the first layer I had ever known of slid away. And now, my mother is the only filter left between having that clear view, finally.

Having had you, it is easier to gaze towards the chasm. You don't have a void or darkness behind your back when you walk in front of your child. I am not the last. I can sense you watching my back as I go. There is nothing lonely about that. Once you have a child, you start looking over your shoulder at what is coming behind, instead of only focusing forward to the last rice-doors between you and the abyss. Suddenly you see instead an infinite line of life behind you, and all is well.

Psychologists tell us that a stage we all have to go through, growing up, is to discover that our parents are not gods. It is a kind of chock to realise that our parents have faults and weaknesses and petty or wholly selfish sides, they say. I never thought my parents were gods when I was a child. I always knew somehow that I could not expect them to have less or more space than I on earth. Now that my father has died, I keep noticing my hands as they move over the keyboard. The little finger on my left hand will not stretch out properly. It never did, just like my fathers. The shape of my fingers are the same too and from the fashion the wrinkles are slowly appearing and how the little finger is getting increasingly crooked, there can be no doubt whose daughter I am. Of course, my father is my creator, and I am formed in his image, like I am in my mothers. "Look at my hands," your babu said, "they look like my mothers did just before she died." Only he could see it and so he decided he was dying, that his time had come. This big, strong, adventurous, argumentative, merciless, yet impossibly soft man left when he felt he had become the image of his dying mother. And so how he was created in the image of his mother and father, he left the image of himself behind when he knew it was quite finished, had arrived at its absolute form. And I stuck myself into his body as pulling a pair of perfectly fitting gloves on, and carried from here a younger version of his hands, his ears, his cheeks, his eyebrows, the tip of his nose and his skin, and then whatever details were left of him, after my sister had taken her parts too, pulled back in to the shadows, to become as naked and invisible as before he was born.

I watch you in the gap between the layers of materials I have hung as curtains in the meshed windows in my canvas walls. I watch you as you start your habitual morning bird-tour with Amedi. Your little ears look pink when the two of you walk straight towards the place where the sunlight is creeping over the foothills of Mount Meru. You can always recognise wing-nut ears when the sun shines through them. I noticed that when I looked at your babu's ears, and I often notice that when I look at myself. One day you will notice it too. You might hate it first, but do nothing about them, please. Don't have them taken in. You might regret it after I am no longer here.

MARCH

There is a storm outside, and Laito went home at three. You are sleeping, totally unaware of the wall of rain outside. Bahati and I are in the kitchen laughing, rushing back and forth. She has hoisted her shocking-pink skirt, made from the same kitenge cloth as her top with puffed sleeves, and her headdress, and made a knot by her knees. She has quite forgotten that she is not strong, as she lifts the whole wood table while I roll away the carpet under it. Sometimes it annoys me a little when she comes and demands a ride to somewhere, while I am in the middle of working. To places where others easily walk. She always explains to me it is because she is too fragile to walk the path to the road, two kilometres away. Other times she laughs when I presume she is strong enough to lift a sack of maize flower from the car, though I carried it there from the market in town. In fact, she tells me she is far too weak to lift anything big, though she sees the rest of us doing it. Now and again, when I sit in my little writing tent, I hear her shrill voice call for Laito's help to lift anything slightly heavier than you. She is at least twenty cm taller than him, is another ten cm broader over the shoulders and carries at least four pounds extra muscle than he. He has the same shoe size as me and she is two sizes bigger than us. But as he is quite unquestioning towards her notion that any man is stronger and tougher than any woman. None of them think this the least unnatural. That I go away and hunt buffalo she shrugs at and laughs at and then ignores. Much like she does when I speak Danish or Swedish. It's all gobbeldygook to her. Patiently, Laito's small body appears when she calls him. She then lifts you off the floor like a little dot of a human being, lumbers out of the room and lets him get on with the heavy lifting. Sometimes I worry a little that she calls him too much, while she sits there playing with you, but he does not look too concerned about any of it.

The water is pouring in and we pull away carpet and put buckets under the worst leaks and mop the floor with towels. Water, I am thinking, gets in everywhere. I wonder if her house ever leaked this much. I am glad that huge leaks seem so natural to her. That it is just something to do something about. I think I want it to keep raining for a while. I want the storm to be so exceptionally large that everything gets wet and we have to give up and sit down with our feet up by the kitchen table and laugh like sisters. That will be one of the occasional excuses for breaking the boss/ employee relationship. I put the kettle on the fire.

Then the rain suddenly stops, and you wake up. Bahati shrieks delightedly and hits her thighs and makes outraged sounds at how violent rains can be. As if they are not always like that. Then she goes up to pick you up from your cot. Minutes later, the sun is shining again. I kiss you ten times at least and tell her I could never possibly cook food for you like she does. How you could never love my food as much as you love hers, and I really don't care if it is true or not. I am just saying things because I am drunk with love for you.

MARCH

You see, I have to ask for your forgiveness already. I could not do it. I could not continue with your father. He loves you deeply. It is just that life does not always lead you in the direction that you think seems obvious. That is not really so sad when you think about it properly. It's the expectations that mess it all up, lie and confuse. Life is just being life.

It is some task to choose and decide upon who we want to be. We rub ourselves against each other emotionally, so it's easy to imagine that manners are therefore contagious. It's easy to tell yourself that hat one person's action can explain the reaction of the other. This is a lie. We have the power to decide who we want to be and stay on course, no matter what happens around us. Sometimes, that means stepping out of the company of a person entirely.

Your brow is wet from sleeping close to my neck. I turn you on your side. You always sleep in my embrace. I tried for a while to put you in your own bed, next to mine, but then one day it suddenly seemed so ridiculous to me. You can sleep with me for as long as you want. No chimpanzee would ever consider going up into one tree, leaving its young there, sliding down and then going over to sleep in the next tree, now would it? There has been enough chaos. I think we still have not understood exactly to what degree simple physical nearness and touch can heal.

I can hear two hyenas calling just outside. The night is still, but the house is shaking a little from an earth tremor. I pull you a little closer again because that sound of hyenas in the night makes me very happy and I want you to feel it too, somehow.

APRIL

Words are an amazing tool for those who use them sincerely, but they can be the greatest hindrance there is if you don't.

Maybe at some stage we all get a past that makes it difficult for us to respond to what another person is trying to convey. We miss each other by millimetres, often perfectly aware of what the other is trying to say, but unable to both admit it, because we are muted by our own fearful emotions and the consequences of accepting things we do not want to hear. When we finally begin to acquire wisdom enough to successfully solve human puzzles, we seem bent on building yet more complex ones. It must be that the true simplicity of it all offends and disgusts us.

We become air when we live entirely to ourselves. I do not mean that in the sense that we cannot have perfectly satisfactory lives living on our own in near isolation. What I mean is that if we do not to receive any words, and if there is no one there to catch the words we send out, we become completely invisible to ourselves. Like bats, we map and build the reality of others. Their shapes become visible to us when they send an echo of our words back to us. From us and back to us. Rarely is there communication. Understanding another is near impossible.

I am working on a story that I look forward to telling you. If ever you read this book, I will quite certainly have told you about it many times already and you will smile to yourself. It is a story about the berry-furry. The berry-furry is a rather nasty creature that sits and waits in strawberry fields, by bramble bushes, raspberry bushes, blueberry bushes, and so on. The berry-furry cannot, for some reason that I have yet to make up, pluck the berries itself, but rely on you to help it satisfy its almost obscene greed for berries. It never asks, instead it swoops in, so fast that you may not notice it, (though of course I saw one on such-and-such an occasion), and steals the berry you have just picked, somewhere between leaving the plant and entering your mouth. It is therefore adamant, when one plucks a strawberry or any of the aforementioned berries, to get it in to the mouth as fast as absolutely, humanly possible.

I am yet to understand what creature swoops in though, between two intelligent people and changes words at some stage during the distance they travel from one person's mouth to another person's ear, and there must be a way to catch and kill that little bastard. I promise I will do my best to catch it before you start talking. But I think people have been trying for thousands of years. My hope is dampened a bit by that.

To try to use words properly is important, though. It is not the abundance of them; the numbers have no relevance. Rather, if you speak, let them be as close a colour print of the picture you carry inside as possible.

Some say that action matters more. I do not want to contradict that, but surely violence starts where lack of words frustrates.

Words that utter our inner thoughts, expressed precisely as they are felt, and received as they were meant, are one of the absolutely only passages—even if it is only momentary—to break our fundamental isolation.

Squandering those silken precious lines between humans, to an insincere or superficial choice of words, or to laziness, is building walls and creating prisons. Big words throw out flippantly—one thing one moment and another the next, criss-crossing in all directions and with no solidity and no clear line of developmental history or direction, brings confusion, pain, or worse, a feeling of betrayal and abandonment. Small words, forgotten, just because they are small, quite extinguish their little lives.

If we do not stand by our words, if we do not mean our words, and will not try to grasp the meaning behind the words of the other, if we keep words from someone whom we know they belong to, or we try to stab reality in the back with false words, then the two humans standing in front of each other turn from soul to some pounds of sound-vibrating flesh.

It is about the opening of doors, to let the inner creatures come out, for the other to see. It is a painful thing to try to fit one key after the next into that hole, in trying to open with words, the doors to these inner pens. It creates misunderstandings that are sometimes irrevocable, hurtful, devastating. So we must keep trying. We must keep forgiving, fine tuning, sharpening, searching for, creating words.

Some words never meant so much to me and always looked like this: **rich and powerful.** Words that to me now look like this: **exciting, intelligent, eloquent** used to be more like **exciting, intelligent, eloquent**. And when I looked at **kind and with a sense of humour**, the other day, I realised it had quite grown to **Kind and with a sense of humour**.

I once gave a word to someone. I took it out of my mind's vocabulary and now it is buried with him to never dress my voice again.

I will have words that are only for you, too. Words that can only be kept alive by your voice.

And then there is the word "sorry". You will hear me say that to you quite a few times in our life together. Those who do not believe in that word see themselves as a god or a devil. I just hope I will choose the right places to say that word to you, because otherwise it won't help anything but my vanity, and any measure of vanity of the soul can never be too small.

APRIL

It is still raining. I put on Frank Sinatra on our small music player, lift you up and dance with you in a waltz-grip, around the little kitchen. You let your head fall back and laugh in every swirl. The water is streaming in from leaks everywhere in the makuti roof. Basins and pots of all colours and sizes are under them and we turn up the music more the harder the rains become.

As soon as the rains stop, I give you to Bahati and go down to my writing tent. A moment later I hear someone calling: "Hodi," and I answer to him to draw near. Situani, the occasional askari who is there when Amadi is on leave, appears in the tent door opening with four slightly wilted sun flowers. He holds them awkwardly, as if he is not sure if they are safe. It is astute of him, for the Waarusha would never normally give flowers as a present, but he has understood that this is something I like to have on my table. He must have seen my reaction to receiving flowers before. I thank him and prompt him to say what it is he wants in return, for I am sure it is something. His explanation does not come with this set of sunflowers, but with the wilted ones he brings me three days later. A problem has occurred, he starts. There is silence for a while. He chased his wife, and she ran into a wall.

"Really?" I say, "ran into a wall? Not even chickens do that."

He nods thoughtfully, as though I've brought up a new perspective. Situani then continues explaining his problem to me in a lighter tone. He needs some thousands of shillings, so he can buy two kilos of sheep's fat. She is refusing to leave her parent's home and come back to him, he tells me, while looking at his toes in his moped tyre sandals. Unless he gives her two kilos of sheep's fat. In fact, she left last Tuesday, eleven days ago.

"You have come to me, a woman, your boss, and ask me for money so you can pay the penalty your wife demands, because you beat her? Are you kidding?"

His chin lifts a bit, and he looks down his nose at me.

"It's not my wife who is demanding this. She has made the elders demand it. Before this time, I did not hit her in six years. For six years, did I not lay a hand on her. It is only a loan. I swear to god I did not hit her for six years. Six years is a long time." I look at him for a long time. He says nothing and corrects his shuka. "I will not hit her again."

There is a silence again.

There is a dust storm outside, and it is a typically cold July day here on the slopes of Mount Meru. It is mid-winter now, and I have forgotten to tell him I will pay for the coal he and Amadi use when they are up here at night with their spears pretending to guard, while really sleeping on a chair, in the outside kitchen. Not much Tanzania about this view today, I think and look out between the canvas door and beyond Situani. A dust devil rotates past us further down. I cannot see any huts from my desk today, I realise I have not even tried until now. They are behind the yellow dust. The view has completely gone. Just a nicotine yellow enveloping us and our entire little hill. Situani's eyebrows and eyelashes are blond from the dust. His shuka lifts with a passing dust devil and he holds it down, hunches his shoulders and steps inside the tent. He puts the flowers down on a stack of books. There is a moment of silence as we listen to the falsetto shrieks of a donkey somewhere near. And then we walk the twenty metres up to my little home and I give him his blood money and remind him to be back at three o'clock tomorrow, as usual.

MAY

Who will you be as a grown woman? What will be your driving force?

I was 29 when I said to myself: "Just let me hunt buffalo now. Please, just let me not be killed, or worse, badly wounded by a buffalo before the age of 40. I will stop when I am 40. If indeed I continue after that, it will be at my own risk. It will be my fault, then."

If ever there was a deal, it is now broken. The cords were severed two years ago.

I try to get away from it sometimes. To stop. I think of the danger. I have moments of great fear when I imagine you without me. Then I try to just walk through a forest for hours, but eventually the longing is back. Walking around aimlessly in the bush is beautiful, but it is still like looking in on my world from the other side of a thick pane of glass. Not hearing it and it not hearing me. It makes me feel like an actor and I have to put my hunting boots back on. Not to kill, that is never the driving force, but to hunt.

I overhear a conversation between people who hunt, but are killers not hunters and I Imagine spitting on the ground they tread on, to get rid of the bitter taste. When I think of those people, I want to unpack my hunting bag and scatter all shades of green amongst the rest of my clothes. To forget about hunting and forget about them.

But soon, not being in the same room as the rest of nature makes me infinitely sad. I want to be close enough to hear the slightest whisper. You can never get that close when you are just a spectator. You must be involved enough to sink in to its entire structure. And the structure of nature is filled to the brim with the possibility of perfect satisfaction for all our senses. Of course it is like this. Our senses were only made to detect the euphoria of nature's beauty and warn us of nature's dangers, in order to make it worth it and to refrain us from doing anything that might cut us short from an existence long enough to serve life, by creating life. The senses are there to catch the hopeful promise and the grim reality that nature is about three things and three things only: glorious birth, stark death and glorious birth.

Maybe I have never seen something so clearly as nature and maybe I have never felt so clearly seen as by nature. Or maybe I fear man more than nature. Nature has no hatred.

JUNE.
I have little to say about falling in love. I wish I did, but I would be making it up. I know when it is there, acutely and with my entire being, but that is not to say I understand it. I feel it, like I feel the strongest wind in my face—here too, I

have little understanding of how it started and where it started and where it is going to. But no, it is not like a wind.

The *falling* in love could be the falling into the universe, a wingless tumbling towards the darkness, or towards the stars. But no, it is not like a rocket shooting off the planet.

It is nothing like a cat either. The cat symbolises something admirably independent and impossible to tame. Something that comes and goes as it pleases, eats out of your hand one day, to disappear for months the next. Yes, a cat also is an animal that smooths itself on you, as it slips between your legs in figures of eight, not caring what rubbish it leaves on your trousers. Then scratches you when you stop to pick it up and kiss it. It is everywhere when you are not looking and nowhere to be seen when you are. The cat it is a survivor and a killer who's mercy you can quite forget when it has the upper hand. One could have thought so, but no, being in love is nothing like a cat.

It is as impossible to hold as water. I know that. It will slip through your fingers and get sucked up by the ground or evaporate when you thought you had it jarred, and it will rise around your feet, upwards in the heat. When it is not forcing its way through your roof, dripping from your ceiling on to everything you have, leaving nothing you have unmarked, un-stained or sacred. But it is not like water either, I suspect.

I don't think I can say something firm about being in love. Nothing. I only ever see what it was from the shiny wrappers it leaves behind; shattered things, forgotten things, lost things, enormously big built things, words of all sizes scattered here and there, beautiful children shooting out of the ground it trod on, whiffs of divinity one moment, the acid stench of piss-fear and a few steps of tango in the grip of suicide, the next.

Still, it is apparent to me that nothing else has anything greater to offer as far as the chase in life goes.

When the sun starts to rise, and the light that went from black to blue turns to grey of day, I might come across a solitary track, just one big track that stands out from sheer size. Half an hour later, as the light sets in strongly, the ground will show a highway of crisscrossing tracks. I know that the one that was clear from the first minute of light, before the others, is the one to follow.

When light sinks again in the late afternoon, and all the sounds mellow out, the mishmash of tracks and the circus of sounds will fade once more. Again, that one big solitary track will stand out for a few minutes before nightfall. One more time for a few minutes it will appear sharper than any other, as if no other significant animals ever passed here.

The times when I spend all I have, but don't catch up with a track like that, I know I followed something that was worth hunting. That's the best a hunter can do.

About love, I can say even less. We try to name it and put together constellations in its name, but I am too submerged too much in its belly and at its mercy to see much above its surface, to comments on what it looks like. Only one sentence springs to mind;

It is, it is, it is, and it is the only thing that is.

JULY

I am thinking that unselfish kindness is a funny one. I struggle to understand how one can do anything entirely selflessly. To me, it is not selfless to share ones food with a hungry person. There is no greater pleasure in the human heart. Lie if you like. It may not be why you do it, but the fact is that you feel good when you have done it. I like a selected few of the Christina ideas, but to me there is nothing selfless in them. I see nothing humble about Jesus. The do-gooders trampling around the globe with the single aim of "giving" might give themselves more than anyone. It may not be meant to be selfish at all, but it still is.

I don't know why it matters so much to me that an act of kindness should be selfless, since it may very well be the result that matters and not the reasons that lie behind it. Yet, we live in a society where motive is important and I too have been influenced by that. Motive makes the difference between murder and manslaughter. But then I look at you, a few months old. Fierce little eyes burning, looking at me, commanding me like a mute animal. So in the end I wonder if the only selfless kindness comes from the wholly unaware person, just from being in someones life. There is no way on earth that you could ever know, or feel smug about the fact, that you fill my being all the way to the brim with love and purpose, just by existing.

AUGUST

Losemingore, Tanzania.
This safari was only ten days. I am up here hunting the
buffalo of the mountains of Losemingore. I cannot go away
for as long as I did the last time. It was a mistake to leave you
for three weeks straight. You see? I might have already hurt
you.

I do not necessarily hope that you will be a hunter, but I have
to show you the depths of the senses.

How ever many times I walk past a wild jasmine up on the
mountains, I pick up on its smell acutely, for my nose is
trying to find the smell of a buffalo. Every time the wind
changes and carries with it something sweet, or the base
stench of rotting flesh, somewhere in a miombo forest in
western Tanzania, a small mental olfactory map builds: "Over
there, where the stench is coming from, there could be lions."
"This smell. We have to turn back. It will rain heavily soon," is
ignored by the smell called "we are near buffalos now." And in
all of that, like a small background instruments to the key
feature are the; "oh that tree is just beginning to blossom," or
"a leopard passed here recently," or "burnt grass somewhere
near here."

Not that you are trying to, but when your eyes are
constantly looking at spoor, there is a world between each of
the steps your quarry left behind. There is a specific grass,
that I do not know the name of, but I know so well, because it
has a minute red spots on it, the same colour as dried blood.

The white butterflies there, one after the other, lift from animal droppings. There the thin line of merciless siafu.

Where the dew is missing in long lines over the grass, speaks silently of a herd of buffalo passing in the night. There the indentation where a bushbuck has slept, and where an elephant has rubbed itself on a tree year after year, or there a bushpig has uprooted and upturned the ground. All these animals that have left signs behind are as visible and truly present to me as if were they there in the flesh and for a few seconds, in between tracks, I wonder where they are now.

When I hunt, my skin is faintly conducting. The skin on my face, ears or neck tells me where the wind is coming from. I try to ignore the giant stinging nettles that burned through my trousers. I relish that it mostly just takes the removal of one stick behind my back to fall asleep under a tree during midday. My left thumb knows so intricately well the spring of the safety catch, knows exactly how to hold it just before it slips on to "fire," when I am in thick bush.

When I do not hear the occasional stout bawl of one buffalo bull telling another to get out of the way, I listen even more intently for a branch that snaps, the rattle of a big body brushing by a dry bush. And on the way to searching out those sounds, a hunter's ears pick up anything and all that they are strong enough to lift. Beetles buzz by, the emerald spotted wood doves call that always seems so far away, the red chested cuckoo always nearer, especially just after it has rained, the honey guide following us like a madman. Two trees, their branches grinding against each other in the wind. A straddler guinea fowl trotting away on dry leaves.

When following a wounded buffalo, the bark of the bushbuck and the sudden flight of the yellow-necked francolin tightens my jaw. And finally, those hoarse, drawn bawls of a dying bull, that I know to be its last, that in that moment brings no pain, only relief.

After that, for a moment, there is a stillness when I wait my twenty minutes before going up to the animal. A stillness that cannot be penetrated by anything but the sound of a buffalo still alive after all.

There is the smell of stomach, the blood, smoke, the fire, and the liver roasting on a stick.

An acquaintance scolded me for hunting buffalo in what is known as one of the most dangerous areas in Tanzania. He says: "Can you just not hunt in the other areas? You have a child now! Why do you insist on going to that place exactly? Why?" What can I answer him? I can only sink my head lower between my shoulders in shame and be quiet. Whatever happens, forgive me, for I do not even understand this longing in me myself. It is some kind of thirst for being part of a world where I am at peace. Try to understand me. It is nothing to do with my love for you. The crew and I set up a fly-camp on the lower end of the ridge. The mist is thick up there right now. Sometimes it does not lift until ten in the morning and there is nothing one can do but to wait. Everything is dense and green and impenetrable on that small chain of mountains. Only at the top, an open strip of grass rolls out in front of you like a chameleon's long tongue and offers clear views and easy walking. On the hunched trees, long moss beards hang down from the branches and bend to the breeze. The turaco dart in and out of the mist and flash their red on the back of their wings.

It is the first time I am on safari since your babu died and I have realised that it will be the first time I come back and will have nobody to talk to about it. It was good to be climbing a mountain when this struck me. It kept the heart pumping confidently.

When an eland bull appears in the lifting mist less than twenty metres from us, I look at the hunting guest but I can see from his face that the only thing he sees is an animal we are not hunting. My chest tightens. I notice I clench my jaw before I walk on. Why does it hurt me so much when people can't see or hear or smell anything? Ten minutes later, the bull appears again. It is facing us now. Then it turns and trots away. I hope it will keep running for a long time. Away from all of this shit, I think angrily. I mentally look for my father's hand on my shoulder and find it there.

The old mans beards on the trees all bend upwards in the lifting wind. Like doddering old fools who keep on living. Beards growing and growing and never seeming to get any longer. Thousands of years of the same old story.

I chase after buffalo in some insatiable hunger. That is what I do, really. I have already tried playing with the thought of stopping this game. Before it becomes my turn to get a horn pushed in between my ribs. Eventually, things happen. They do to most hunters.

I see his face, see how it looked after he had died. My first thought, when I saw it, was that my sister had arranged his face before I got there. To make it prettier. It was as if he was making one of those silly grins he used to do when he wanted to show us he was not falling for that poor excuse. I will not forget her for that generous action and like it even better because I think I know what he would have looked like when she did it. I can see the almost childish movement of her fingers. The fear on her face. He probably did not look so different dead from what he looked like when he fell asleep in front of the television. His mouth wide open. Except he would have had open eyes. And I always knew, because I tried it on a dead red deer at home, when I was little, that to close his eyelids would have not been such an easy task at first. To me, he went to the flames with my sister's fingers all over his face. She would have been the last one to kiss him before he died. That helps a little. I did not make it in time. "not make it in time" for a person who never waves once, but always turns around one last time.

Walking up and down the mountains looking for an old buffalo bull, days in and days out, I look for the feeling of his hand on my shoulder. Your babu went to the grave with the other half of a code to the gate of our world. An entire world behind a massive door has been reduced to what anybody getting close enough can see through a keyhole. Fragments of hunting scenes, weather, milky teas in frosty weather when I was tiny, the beginning of the art of silence for a small girl, the overwhelming awe of nature and two people seeing the same thing and seeing each other, seeing them. But now it can only be had in fragments. Sentences in a story that even you are likely to become impatient with at some stage.

The guest shoots. We follow a wounded buffalo for days. It stays with the herd. I see this already in the first hour of tracking it. It is still alive and will continue to be so. We walk through nettles and green shrubs that swallow us up in confused darkness. We follow it for three days, but it is only getting stronger. It is a superficial wound only. It has almost stopped bleeding. Pin sized drops. Still, we follow it. Then it rains. Torrential rains open up and everything is wiped clean. Even the Tracks. We eventually give up. I do not want to and feel sick about it, but there is nothing more to be done. The safari is ending and the permit will not allow me to stay there for another day. Eventually we come off the mountain too and we come back to the main camp, an hour's drive away from the mountain.

I have my first proper shower in a week. We have dinner and I pull the crispy sheets over my legs. I am not so tired, but utterly still. I watch the moon through the mesh of the canvas tent. To lose a wounded animal, is the most shameful thing that can happen to a hunter. I have failed.

I fall asleep quietly and only wake up with the doves the next morning. My left eye stings this morning. My left eye, the one you scratched with a sharp little nail when you were only four months old, still stings and weeps for the first hour in the morning. Often, I sit on my camp bed in the dark at five in the morning, sometimes with my gun-belt in my hand and wait for the sting to go away, so I can open it and go out to meet the hunting guest for breakfast. Often it is still weeping through breakfast. I should have never told the tracker what happened to my eye. Immediately he told me it weeps whenever you are missing me. It weeps for me to remember you at home. Now, of course, I might never see that doctor.

My next thought is whether I should not just go out on the veranda, still wearing my striped kanzu, my tent is far away from the others. I decide to get dressed instead.

I sit here, my little love, thinking about these last days of hunting those mountains. Walking up and down and across the flat ridges on top when I felt, or imagined, the weight of your babu's hand on my shoulder the whole time. He was young and strong again. His long legs, lean and muscular. Like they used to be.

I put my .458 Lott, on the table in front of me. Set out all the barrel cleaner, the gun oil, the stock oil. The barrel has got some tiny specks of rust from the wet days on the mountain. How quickly the rust comes. The notch in the stock of my gun is so visible still. I rub it as if it will go away, though I know perfectly that it will not. When that happened, your babu was still alive. It was the last safari I did while he was alive still.

When I saw him last, I sat by the side of his bed and told him stories from that safari. You were there too. You were sleeping in the guest-room and I was sitting on the floor next to his bed. He asked me to tell him stories from that safari and he held on to my hand in a fashion he had never done before. Wanting reassurance from my hand. He looked at me with big sunken brown eyes, and asked me to tell another one. And I did. His face looked at mine as if he was saving a bit of it, for later. The last story I told him was about the two buffalos that came straight at me and my guest when they got our wind just about twenty metres away. But he seemed to enjoy my voice more than my story. He had never done that before. He did not ask enough about the details. Like he should have.

Now I will keep that notch there. Ishmael will have to age, too. With warts and all. Ishmael is my longest living witness to my life in the bush. Others have been with me on some safaris, many maybe. But Ishmael has been with me every time. Just like your babu was waiting to be filled in on the telephone about the entire safari every time I got back to the hill. Ishmael, his wooden body and his metal skeleton, knows, though he is deaf and dumb. But I will not remove his scars now. It would seem like a lie.

I rub away the superficial rust on the barrel and wonder if you will ever hold this gun, or rest it over your shoulder, as you walk through the bush. In a way, I hope not. It is a bloody awful affair in so many ways and in my twenty years, I have to this day met less than a handful of gentlemen in this business.

Your babu, at the time I was struggling the most to become a buffalo hunter here in Tanzania, phoned me and said that he was sorry that he had given me such an impossible dream, by bringing me up the way he had.

But dreamless, we wake and live restless and confused.

AUGUST

Oldonyo sambu

It is twenty minutes before your bedtime and I walk outside with you. It is only you and I on the hill. I am not sure why Amadi, your favourite bird-guide, is not here. We take a walk and you sit like a little arrow on my left arm as we walk up the steep hill, behind our home. Three Masai women come down from that which was a forest just a few years back, carrying big stacks of wood on their backs, straps across their foreheads. They are in a hurry to get back home before it gets dark. You wave and when they see it, they stop and shout to me I should give you to them. I can just have another one. Please, just give us this one, they call. I shout back that they can bring me two of theirs and we will make a deal. They laugh and shout back that it is a deal. Then they keep walking on down the hill. Donkeys and goats and cattle herded by children come past below us as well. You point out the obvious as the animals disappear downward one by one. It will be dark soon. It does not really look so right now, but in twenty minutes the sun will have gone. Sunset is fast here. Maybe tonight I will have you in my arms all night. Just because there will be a lifetime of you sleeping without me next to you later.

I wonder if we will go down to Lake Tanganyika next week. You and I and Bahati and look for that man-eating crocodile. I should like us to. We would be together during the day. I would write a little and Bahati would be there to play with you. I am sure we could find somewhere to swim where it is safe. The water is crystal clear in Lake Tanganyika. We are still waiting for the local DC to give us the permission by letter. He might have a last-minute regret of letting a white person do such a thing. I have told my friends, the ones who asked us to come down and help them with it, not to let them know I am a woman.

My letter, The half-hearted permission I and all the other profession hunters are given every year, that lets me operate for a season at a time only, always starts: "Dear sir," so no one will know. No one will know if Natasha is the name of a man or a woman. Once I am down there, what can they do? They will not stop us then. Not if I come with my gun and rid the village of a crocodile that ripped the arm off a little girl just the other week. Why do I want this so much? Because I am a do-good'er, who cares desperately about the villagers around Lake Tanganyika? No, not more than most aid-workers do when they pack their bags and leave a dark Swedish town to go the bush in Africa somewhere. No, I am afraid that it is not the main reason. Though the outcome will be good for all, the main reason is that I want to have a history with you. I want to build roots in the air. I have no land anymore to offer you. All the family land in Europe, all the fortunes, were lost. All I can do is build a history for us. This will, however, be stronger than any dirt, than any crop or acreage. It is the only thing I can promise you. That we will have a lot of history together. That is all. I don't know what it will be yet. How can I? I know it will be a history full of a mother's love and a mother's faults and shortcomings. But it will be the best I can do. I give you my word upon that.

SEPTEMBER

I put you into your little bed, next to mine. As I stood over you while you slept, I put my hand on your fast beating heart. I have never felt so grateful in my life. Then I went and sat by my small coal fire in our kitchen for a moment, to taste and wallow in my wealth properly for a moment. The embers burn steadily in the clay fire stead.

Then, like a knock on the door, I remember. Today I was told two things. Three men were eaten in one go in a hunting camp, I know. Lionesses. And That there is a gang of men on mopeds that have gone on a rampage shooting women drivers in Arusha. I feel sad for those people and the families of those who were eaten, but lions have no hatred. It is hatred that makes me want to vomit. I feel sick, too much information at once, but I know I must just do what one must do if one wants to stay on this continent; Make a reasonable plan, keep your eyes and ears open, keep all senses open, make a reasonable plan again, and then just get on with it without wasting too much energy on fear.

Gripped by a sudden worry, I go back to your bed again. The lamps are flickering. I forgot to buy kerosene. There you are. You are sleeping soundly. Arms and legs are wide apart, suggesting all corners of the world to whomever might ask for directions. I have something important to ask of you, I whisper. I cannot have an opinion on what you do with your soul or your mind. But your body, your flesh, I ask you to look after it. To take care of it, guard it intelligently. To keep it alive and well. Your body, my love, was made by mine. You grew surrounded by my soft flesh. You are my pip. Your body is my root to earth, as is mine for my mother. I close the mosquito net around your bed and take a few steps, then I turn around, go back and pick you up and take you to my bed.

I never understood, until now, how much pain I must have put my mother through, being in the tracks of buffalos so often. She must have feared for the safety of my body. Never did she mention it in all the years. She must have feared ringing telephones at odd hours, more than most mothers.

SEPTEMBER

Dar es Salaam, Tanzania.

We have had to travel south in Tanzania for a couple of days. We fly to Dar es salaams to attend a meeting with some of the other hunters. In a hot hotel room, we fall asleep in one bed. The past of my father, the past with your father and the future of you and the grey mist souls of the dead elephants, restless images intermingling, wake me up from night terrors. They are getting worse, I think as I get up and close the window to the loud muezzin shouting his faith at the blueing light of dawn. The heat is thick. The fan is racing over the sagging mosquito net. You sleep soundlessly in the middle of the double bed. Your blonde hair is sticking to your sweaty brow and your arms and legs are splayed wide to both sides, as is your habit. You look like a broad fat starfish of trust.

I go back to sleep again, and the worst nightmare, one that makes something shift in me, is about trumpeting elephants running wild. Coming in the hundreds towards me. My father running naked and bleeding, you riding the elephants. Copies of you, one sitting on each elephant. All the "you's" are naked. When one elephant is shot in the knee, at first it wobbles, then it falls to the ground like a coat falling off a hanger, just an empty grey skin, soulless, fleshless. In the dream, I know they are the elephants my grandfather filmed in the Sudan in the 1920ies. They are the exact elephants from his film. Did they really live for this long? I think to myself. But that is amazing. I see I am the elephant at the front, the one who was shot in the knee. All the little copies of you are strewn on the ground around the battleground, but all they all crawl away unharmed. I cannot see my father, but I know he is dead. The sorrow is boundless. In the dream I whisper:

Trumpet, then elephant, the big stride so vain,
Uproot with its trunk, a trunk of a tree.
Yet, a crumbling pillar in the rain
When merely wounded to the knee.

DECEMBER

Oldonyo sambu.

A few weeks have passed. Nothing much has happened in those weeks. It seems the dust devils in the Rift Valley spin slower, slower, until they stop and fall mid-twirl, like a wind-up toy. No storm has shaken our house for a while. There is no rain. No earth tremors. The nights are crisp and all sounds for a wide radius around us are clear. Then one morning I wake up and know that something new has begun. I feel the strength of it wash in, as I throw you up in the air and watch you laugh. It is back, and it feels stronger than ever before. "Infinite possibilities" are back. Oh, they are here to stay for a long time.

I have been neck bent, on my knees, three or four times in my life so far. It is always to do with love or death. Nothing else got me until now. But how it gets me, when it does. That is when life feels like Glass-en-route-concrete-travel.

Then one day it rolls on, out of nowhere. It hoists itself like a sail in the pit of my stomach and I stand up again, ready to receive anything from a hot gust of wind to polar storms.

When the biggest visitor of all, "Infinite possibilities" arrive, you know clearly that there is more beauty, more love, more books, more pain, more fights, more meaning, more dirt. There is more of something grand that you don't know what is, but know that you are supposed to be part of, and it feels hugely exciting and mysterious and certain.

The times will come in your life where you will feel hope is lost. It may last for a while. But just wait, "infinite possibilities" are suddenly there exploding out of your chest, with that same mysterious strength of dandelions pushing through concrete. Then there is a sounding horn in the pea soup fog that tells you something is about to move out, and that you too can be on board if you just get up now, and keep walking towards the sound. No, run! Towards it, get on it, while the tide is high!

It is not momentary. Now it begins.

Now finally, I have all the luggage I need to carry us through any weather, and any land, and your little hand is in mine. And beginnings and ends and new januaries are near.

We are in the middle of the pulsating mess of life together.

Here.

Now.

I give you here a little box. I will give it to you physically one day, but I will also give it to you here. Things have a tendency to get lost, faster than words.

It has two sides that are hollow, deep, and covered in thin glass. A two-sided box that opens like a fat novel in the middle. I am not sure what kind of wood it is made of yet. Maybe walnut on one side and acacia on the other

On one side, there is a butterfly and on the other, there is a note. The butterfly will be spectacular. It can even be a moth, one of those orange and brown and white moths that come past us up here now and again and die by one of the kerosene lamps. On the other side, there is a note. On it I have written: "Those who do not understand that a moment is a perfect entity in itself, do not truly recognise the life of this creature."

I might even put a looking glass there in the box. A tiny little one on a stick that easily slips in and out of a little holder next to the note. Just to make sure you miss none of the colours and the perfection the tiny scales of the wings offer, or how fascinating its face looks, if you look closely enough. Make sure that you will take a proper look at it all. Try to notice every little detail perfectly before your time here runs out.

If it sounds like a cliché to you that happiness lies in taking a mole for a walk, having tea and biscuits on a silver tray with the rabbits and us wearing big hats on Sundays, going for morning picnics in the middle of mist as thick as the lies in the fairy tales I make up for you while peeling your boiled egg, making pocket pets out of field mice, shouting "good night" to Mount Meru before bedtime, eating buffalo heart stew and mashed potatoes while my hunting hat tells you what it has seen, finding fairies in the fire together while a storm rages outside and rattles our little home, or making kerosene lamp shadow theatre on the canvas walls, until you fall asleep in my arms… then it is only because when you read this you have still not become old enough to remember how we laughed or how your eyes widened with passion, or compassion, or adventure. Cliches are just truths repeated to those who simply refuse to listen to any goddamn important thing.

Wherever you are in your life, when you read this, go as soon as you can and stand by a window facing the sea and throw the shutters open at first light. You will never experience a greater earthly power than that. Every time you do that, you will know that all will be how it should be. That all will be well.

I will stop talking here now. You will have to grow a bit more first. I will too. Then later, we will revisit and reassess again. I look forward to the day you can answer me back.

Here is to the day I say "so long." No one gets away with living in the end. But don't worry too much about that, if you can, because the eternity of non-existence, as it was before we were born, surely, is no shorter than the eternity that we encounter again after death. We fear the non-existence that comes after life, but rarely consider the completely improbable, the quite unbelievable fact, that we somehow managed to take form and step out of nothingness for some time.

The life we are given is an exception to the rule.

There are some things you have to do, even if they
scare you. Otherwise you are not a human being,
but just a little shit.

Astrid Lindgren

Thank you Upepo, my friend. Elephants don't forget, and neither will I.